The Motor Coaching Bible

A Dogma for RV Enthusiasts with very little Heresy and almost no Blasphemy

Dave Galey + Friends

Winlock Galey
26135 Murrieta Road
Sun City, Ca 92585

The Motor Coaching Bible

A Dogma for RV Enthusiasts with very little Heresy and almost no Blasphemy

Dave Galey
+
Friends

Published by: Winlock Galey
26135 Murrieta Road
Sun City, Ca 92585

Library of Congress Catalog Card Number:
99-90077

ISBN: 1-890461-14-8 Price: $24.95US

Warning-Disclaimer

This book is designed to provide information only on the subject matter covered. It is sold with the understanding that the publisher and author are not engaged in rendering legal, accounting, engineering, or other professional services. If legal or other expert assistance is required, the services of a competent professional should be sought.

It is not the purpose of this manual to reprint all the information otherwise available to the author and/or publisher, but to complement, amplify and supplement other texts. You are urged to read all the available material, learn as much as possible about motor coaching and to tailor the information to your individual needs.

Every effort has been made to make this manual as complete and as accurate as possible. However, there may be mistakes both typographical and in content. Therefore, this text should be used only as a general guide and not as the ultimate source of motor coaching. Furthermore, this book contains information on motor coaching only up to the printing date.

The purpose of this manual is to educate and entertain. The author and ***WINLOCK GALEY*** shall have neither liability nor responsibility to any person or entity with respect to any loss or damage caused, or alleged to be caused, directly or indirectly by the information contained in this book.

If you do not wish to be bound by the above, you may return this book to the publisher for a full refund.

Contents

Acknowledgments

I want to thank all those who contributed to this work. A special thanks to Sheila Donigan who I regard as a truly unique individual. And, thanks to my old friend, George Thornhill, whose company we have enjoyed on many travel adventures.

Ian Giffin, a new friend on the cutting edge of a new technology, the Web, thanks. And, I can't forget Dick Wright, one of the sharpest and most considerate people I have ever known. And thanks to George Myers, a new author and a respected member of the RV community. Thanks also to Lon Cross and John Miller who unselfishly gave me their input.

I want to thank Jerry Mullins of Creative Printing for his help and patience in putting this book together.

Proof reading was done by my wife, Roberta, and a fellow bus nut and retired English professor, Bob Peck, who currently lives aboard his boat.

Preface

I have no doubt that about every three or four years, a how-to book is published for the RV public. With that disclaimer, I herewith present my own. This is a book of instructions, which if followed closely, will guarantee a successful RV experience (whatever that is).

I am so confident of the material contained herein, I will personally issue my personalized check for the full purchase price as a refund under the following conditions: 1) You must have had a bad RV experience my book did not cover. 2) You are greatly disappointed in the material in the book. 3) You don't like the type font. 4) You think I am ugly. . . Or, 5) You think you paid too much for the book. AND, you are willing to have any or all of the above facts made public and attested to by a justice of the supreme court, a justice of the peace, a notary public or your spouse, and you return the book in pristine condition without a single dog ear, within 24 hours of purchase, so it may be passed on to another potentially dissatisfied buyer.

To be so bold as to write a set of instructions for motor coaching is almost like writing a book about how to reside in your own home. Everyone has all the answers they need from childhood, right? It is not only second nature, it is first nature! We all know how to go to bed, get up, bathe, scrub teeth, flush the toilet, get dressed, eat, etc.,etc. So, why a set of instructions for such a mundane activity? The answer is, we have a few unique surprises it would be nice to be aware of, hence, my justification for this informative and useful tome.

The reader will be lead through a myriad of equipment and information options and sources, techniques for driving and towing, and rules of the road (both legal and moral). We will further explore camping, camping clubs and associations. Full time living aboard an RV is discussed and the many things available to ease and enhance this adventureare also discussed. Furthermore,a vast array of technical toys will be presented for consideration.

We will run the gamut of camping. No doubt, the first camper sought the shelter of a cave or a rock overhang. As mankind matured, a tent was invented to become a portable cave. Later, wheels were added to this portable cave. This wheeled cave was towed by beast of burden and later, by a pick up truck. Finally, we disposed of the trailer and mounted the cave directly on the pickup. Ultimately, the truck was refined into a gorgeous, luxurious and awesome motor coach!

Occasionally, I call upon experts in their field to write a chapter for me. They have done this selflessly with no thought of

remuneration; only the satisfaction of getting their message across and seeing their name in print. The people selected are verbose and always eager to help a novice. They are known nationally and have achieved a degree of fame, thus their qualifications for inclusion in the book.

Those of you, who, having read this book, desire to add to or dispute some contention, are invited to submit your comments which will be duly reviewed and rejected. Just kidding! From this approach, I hope to enhance and expand this book and everyone participating will be classified as an expert in his/her field. You get the credit; I get the cash!

Dave Galey, 1999

Introduction

The term RV, an acronym for recreational vehicle, has become a catchall for several forms of activity. And, is, in fact, a misnomer in many cases. RVs are used by many as a means of livelihood such as vendors at swap meets hawking their ware. Others, in the entertainment business, employ the RV as an on-the-road hotel. While some use their RV as their permanent home.

Therefore, we have four basic uses for the recreational vehicle. They are: 1) Camping, 2) Touring, 3) Gathering, and 4) Dwelling. These are all separate and distinct activities, but in an RV, the experiences are similar.

Perhaps the most basic of these activities is camping. The RV has added an immense degree of luxury to camping. I recall my days in the Army when a pup tent, occupied by two men, a wool OD sleeping bag, a mess kit and a small shovel was the sum of all the camping equipment on hand. Today, the rugged outdoor type can park his coach next to a stream, sleep in a Queen size bed, prepare a meal on his/her Gaggenau range, take a shower with hot water and watch Seinfeld re-runs on television. Some camping experience!

Probably one of the strongest motivating factors towards the use of a motor coach is the concept of touring. With the high cost of hotels and motels, traveling in a motorhome offers many advantages. Not only do we save the cost of hotels and restaurants, we have the convenience allowing our clothes to remain in our own closet and choosing whether to eat our own cooking or dine out. Often, when underway, we may park for the night in a convenient location. when and where we wish without the need for reservations.

When buying an RV, one of the activities least considered is gathering, camp-outs, or rallies. Most people buy a coach or trailer with the idea of traveling or camping. After a trip or two, it is discovered that the unit sits in the driveway or a storage yard most of the time while we are earning a living. In an effort to utilize the coach more, a natural inclination is to join a club or form an association with other like-minded owners and meet for socializing. Thus, we have week-end rallies or camp-outs. Generally, these are held at locations within a few hours travel time from home and include such mundane activities as chip and dips, happy hour and local sightseeing. This provides more justification for owning such a vehicle.

Finally, many couples who have raised their families and disposed of their large house, move into a motor coach to minimize their sphere of responsibility and broaden their options. They move into their RV and live there on a full time basis. Often, a summer will be spent in the front of a son or daughter's house and a winter in Arizona, Florida or Mexico. This nomadic lifestyle offers many freedoms from child-rearing and earning-a-living days.

The purpose of this book is to be a reference manual for all aspects of the RV lifestyle. You will be lead through such mundane items as a list of magazines and their specialties. A list of associations, organizations and clubs will also be provided. Various types of rigs will be discussed and where and how they may be obtained.

We will talk about the operation of these rigs and the associated rules and statutes pertaining to them. Towing will be given a prominent discussion. Suggested check lists are shown for getting underway, breaking camp, towing and returning. Rules of the road and driving tips are listed. Various electronic motoring toys are described. Most of these toys were not in existence just a few years ago. Major state, federal and local parks are listed along with their locations. An appendix containing useful information is also included.

Equipment

The basic camp dwelling unit is the tent (how droll!). This collapsible unit was then packed on our back, or an animal's back and became a portable house. The earliest full timers must have been and still are, the Nomads of the world. As we got smarter and invented the wheel, more permanent tents were built on wagons so, it was unnecessary to fold our tents and slip away. Instead we would hook them up to our ass and roll.

More recently, our ass was replaced

with a motor installed in a pickup truck. So all we had to do was get in and slam the door, crank 'er up, hold on and shut up (a little engraved message given to me by my daughter to mount on my pickup.)

We now had choices, (and still do) as to whether to put the cart before the pickup or behind. As we get smarter and smarter, we tend to put the cart before the horse, so to speak. I'll explain what I mean. Lets play like the pickup is the modern horse. Our permanently erected tent, or trailer, is pulled by our pickup. The next smart thing we did was to mount the tent on top of the pickup so all we had was one unit. This was a good thing because we had less tires and licences to buy. Beside, occasionally, our hitch came loose and we tooled down the road without our dwelling unit; pretty embarrassing!

The next level of smartness was to make the pickup bigger so we could stand up in it and walk back to use the toilet after we swapped drivers on the go. Don't try this in a travel trailer. This was a major advancement over the conventional camper. So now we had to come up with designations such as Class A, Class C, blah, blah. Talk about class warfare! Ultimately, some really smart guy decided to use the body of a bus to make a camper and to date, this is the snazziest thing we got going on ten wheels.

Whoops! (another way of spelling oops!), we have a problem Houston. Back when we were pulling our permanent tent behind our pickup, we would make camp and remember we forgot the beer. Disaster?, no problem. . . just disconnect the pickup and go to the nearest 7-11 and get a six pack of Bud. Now, just try to maneuver a 45 foot bus in and out of a 7-11 parking lot. So now we have come the complete circle. The cart is before the horse in the form of a little tow car (the horse). So now we have to drag this little Toad, more tires, more tolls and more licenses. The major relief is, if we can afford a bus instead of a pickup, all the extra expenses are just a nuisance, not a problem.

The Tent

What can be said about the humble tent? It has been known as a Tepee, Wigwam, a Hogan, and even a two-man shelter-half. But, since a tent has no wheels and no motor, it may not be classified as a motor coach and, therefore, does not belong in this discussion. 'Nuff said about tents, unless you heard the one about the Indian who told his psychiatrist he dreamed he was two wigwams and what did it mean? The psychiatrist said, "You're too tense."

Trailers

Trailers are aptly named since that is just what they do, they trail. Trailers can be as simple as a box trailer with a pop up tent to a sophisticated travel trailer with all the luxuries of home.

The *fifth wheel* is a trailer towed by a heavy duty pickup where the hitch portion of the trailer is inside the bed of the truck. This has the same configuration of a semi-truck, tractor/trailer rig.. Many *fifth wheel* RVs are huge, measuring up to 45 feet in length. Their luxury can rival the most luxurious bus conversion. It is common today to have one or more slide out rooms. This is where a section of the body will extend laterally, similar to a cabinet drawer, but of a size to accommodate a dining area or a sofa or both. Often a section of the bedroom will extend permitting a Queen size bed and

room to walk around the bed. The slide out concept has become very popular recently since the maximum width of our trailer is limited to 102 inches. Anything over that width requires a moving permit with pilot cars in most states. The slide out room can expand the practical width of a trailer up to an additional five or six feet. In the future, I predict a trailer with slide-outs, slide-ups and slide-overs rivaling the appearance of a space station.

The Camper

We are now approaching the motor coach. The camper is a rigid tent siting on a pick up truck. And, as such, it may be removed so the truck might be use as a truck. To bring the idea to a logical conclusion, the rigid tent should become a permanent part of the truck and be designed so the driver and passenger may rise and move to the rear without first exiting the vehicle. With this ultimate aim achieved, we now have the motor coach, sometimes known as a motorhome. We must distinguish between a motorhome and a mobile home. One is mobile and does have a motor while the other is fixed and might have once been a trailer. But, in the vernacular of American slang, a mobile home is not mobile and a motorhome in fact, does have a motor. Is there any sense in all that?

The Motor Coach

Finally, after wasting a number of pages on trivia, we arrive at the subject of this book: the motor coach. This term encompasses everything from the smallest

Cortez motorhome to the 45 footer, 102 wide, double decker bus conversion with slide out rooms and roof deck patio.

This is a vehicle that has it all! It is completely self-contained. I remember as a young man following the hostilities, the arrival of Japanese merchant ships to our shores. Each one of them had a name which ended in Maru (obviously a Japanese word). Always, the ship would have a two, or more, word name. One which comes to mind is *Virginia Maru.* After inquiring of my Japanese friends, I learned a ship is a self contained vessel and the word Maru means whole, complete, circular, without end. Thus the word Maru suggests an entity which stands alone and needs no outside nurturing. Voila. . . the motor coach!

To suggest the motor coach is self contained, means it needs no support from out side sources. It has it's own source of power for heating, electricity, locomotion, cooking, sleeping, entertainment and, in general, anything needed for all the comforts of home. The motor coach needs no sewer since it carries it's own septic system with it.

Back in the early days when a train had all the comforts of home, the sewage from the train's restroom was dumped on the tracks as it sped across the country side.HORRORS! As a general rule, the toilet rooms were locked when the train arrived at a depot. This inspired a famous song I recalled my mother singing while I was a kid. It went to the tune of *Humoresque*:

Don't you know you must refrain
From flushing the toilet while the train
Is standing in the station:
I love you. . . .

The very thought of this practice now would give the environmentalist apoplexy. In fact, this practice, in yachts as small as 15 feet in length, was common as recently as 25 years ago. The sea-cock was used to dispose of sewage while at sea and was frowned upon if done while at your slip. Now, however, all yachts have holding tanks, as do motor coaches, but these tanks must be pumped instead of dumped. Gravity is neat. Aren't you glad you got a land yacht now?

To continue the description of the self-containment features of the motor coach, next we have heat. Comfort heating can be accomplished in several ways. Fuel for heating can be propane (the most common), or diesel fuel. Although gasoline may

be used for heating fuel, we seldom find gasoline fired heaters for installation in motor coaches. Coal is almost never used and the same can be said for wood. The reason I say almost, is I have a friend who installed a tiny wood burning fireplace in his coach. It was mostly for character and ambience, but it really works. Plus, his coach has a slide-out room so there is plenty of space.

Most motor coaches use propane for comfort heat. Perhaps the best propane heating system uses a baseboard heating technique, whereby hot water is circulated through finned radiators and the room is heated through natural convection of the air currents. As the cool air impinges upon the hot fins, it takes on heat and becomes less dense and thereby, rises, sucking in more cool air over the hot fins, creating a circulation.

One of the most desirable features of this form of heating is the absence of noisy fans, or blowers inside the living area. The hot water is generated by a small propane fired boiler and a circulating hot water pump. The system is controlled by a thermostat so the boiler ignites on signal thus maintaining a comfortable inside temperature. The principle drawback to this form of heating is the scarcity of baseboards in a motor coach.

A more common form of comfort heating is the forced air furnace. The forced air furnace is somewhat inefficient in that the heat exchanger tubes are heated with burners and the products of combustion must be exhausted overboard. Therefore, a significant percentage of the heat created by the fuel is dumped. On average I would guess the forced air furnaces are less than 50 percent efficient. This means, each pound of fuel contains a specific number of BTU, and the force air unit delivers only about half of those BTU.

A very efficient propane heater is the catalytic unit. An unvented catalytic heater can cause the consumption of the available oxygen, thus sort of defeating it's purpose. That is, one must allow the area to be vented allowing the cold air to come in. However, a vented catalytic heater is very efficient. The vented heaters have a tiny blower wafting the products of combustion overboard through a flexible duct about the size of a vacuum cleaner hose. Furthermore, this vented heater may be thermostatically controlled, rendering it the best of all choices. What is the draw back? The principle downside to this form of heat is the wall space which must be occupied plus the fact all combustibles must be kept a safe distance away.

The diesel fired heat system is very similar to the first propane system mentioned. They may both employ convective radiators and radiators with small blowers to distribute the heat. An additional convenience to the hot water heating system using both propane and diesel fuel, is a that circuit may be added to provide hot water for bathing and cooking, plus a circuit for pre-heating the engine, for starting in cold weather. One drawback to the diesel fired boiler, is the noise generated by both the burner and the distribution pump. Thoughtful design can solve this problem, however.

Electrical heat is available in the form of toe-kick heaters. These are thermostatically controlled heaters only 3 inches high and about 18 inches wide which fit under the toe-kick area of a cabinet such as a kitchen counter or bathroom Pullman cabinet. Normally they are rated at about 1,000 watts and the thermostat is built in to the face of the unit. These are a very practical source of heat when the coach is plugged into a land line, also known as shore power (borrowing a term from the yachting community).

While we are on the subject of ambient comfort, air conditioning is the next item to discuss. Technically, heating is air conditioning, but in this case we will use the term to mean reducing the inside temperature to something less than the outside temperature. In a desert climate with it's low level of humidity, evaporative cooling is practical. These are also known as swamp coolers since they tend to create a muggy atmosphere one would find in a swamp. Most RV coolers are of the refrigeration type, whether they are a single roof mounted unit or a split unit.

The refrigeration type cooler operates by passing inside air over cooling coils which extract the heat from the air. These coils are then chilled with circulating refrigerant after the refrigerant expels it's heat through an exhaust blower to the outside. In a way, you might say the outside heat becomes hotter by the equipment sucking the heat out of the coach. But, we have the whole outside world as a heat sink, so we are not in any danger of getting the outside too hot. I might add that refrigeration cooling on a boat is much more efficient since the ocean is a much more effective heat sink, that is, it can suck up heat a lot faster than the outside air can.

The principle type of cooling for a motor coach is the roof air conditioning unit and the split airs. The advantage of the roof mounted unit is it's efficiency and cost. If something goes haywire with it, simply toss it and mount a new unit with little effort. It does have the disadvantage of being unsightly, or ugly as some might say. And, the blower for delivering the cool air and exhausting the hot air, requires more volume than a split unit. Hence the noise factor can be very annoying.

The split refrigerated air conditioning units generally mount the condenser and the compressor in the baggage compartment or below the floor line. This way the only noise we encounter is the circulating fan as it blows over the evaporator. The principle problem with split units is disposing of the heat developed in the condenser. This is customarily done by using a blower of suf-

ficient volume to dump it overboard (again a nautical term).

A commonly overlooked item of bodily comfort in a motor coach is the awning. Most people regard the awning as a neat little sun shade so they can sit outside and enjoy their drinks as long as the deer flies aren't biting. If I had a choice of one patio awning or window awnings all around, my choice would be the window awnings. Why, you ask? Often, you would like a little breeze wafting through your coach but the window shades block off the air. You can feel the breeze if you lift your shades but then the sun comes boiling in canceling the benefit. The answer is to extend your window awnings so you can enjoy ocean air but not the burning sun.

Most coaches will have a full size shower and bathroom. Holding tanks are large enough to stay away from facilities for weeks. The fresh water plumbing is similar to a normal residence. Hot water may be provided with a separate propane fired water heater or, as mentioned earlier in the discussion about heating. Water filters are commonly included for drinking water, cooking and ice making. Obviously, the water cannot be delivered by gravity as in most homes. So a pump is needed to maintain water pressure. In addition to the storage tank and the pump, a hydraulic accumulator is needed to eliminate pulsing and maintain uniform water pressure. This is nothing more than an air spring; a tank partially filled with water and air trapped above the water level which absorbes the pressure changes as the pump pulses.

The electrical conveniences of the modern motor coach not only include a motor driven generator but a battery driven inverter. This allows the occupants to enjoy all the normal electrical devices in their coach as they would in their home. This means it is unnecessary to seek out appliances designed only for direct current. Any appliance which will work in a home may now be transferred to the motor coach. In fact, another advantage to this is that lighting fixtures for the home provide much more variety than those designed only for the RV industry. Conventional TV and stereos may be enjoyed in the coach. And, If you have a small satellite dish at home, it may be disconnected and brought along on your trips in the coach. This is often done by simply mounting the dish on a square of plywood and clamping it to a convenient place on the motorhome. Of course many of the newer motor coaches have permanently mounted remote controlled satellite dishes on their roofs.

For most applications, the inverter is sufficient. When running the air conditioning, however, power supplied by the generator is mandatory unless one is plugged into shore power. Many of the modern motor coaches are all electric which means 120 volt AC power must be available to operate the refrigerator, the oven and the cook-top unit. These coaches must have large battery capacity to allow the inverter to supply these systems. In addition, the generator must be run periodically to recharge this large battery source.

Electronic gadgets abound. We have the GPS, global positioning satellite receivers which tell us exactly where we are at any time. They even let us know we are at home when we are. Isn't that neat? It used to be we had to use a device as primitive as a road map and all we really knew was we were somewhere between Oklahoma City and Tulsa. Now, with certitude, we can declare we are 32.34 miles from Tulsa and our ETA is 29.063547 minutes. Boy! That's impressive!

More electronic gadgets are the computer, the cell phone, and the Internet. With all these electronic toys, we might tend to become a little distracted from our principle job which is to rubber-neck and enjoy the scenery and be a tourist and dump the tank and change a tire if necessary.

Almost all larger motor coaches, including bus conversions, have diesel engines for the main power plant. Now, this is a subject all it's own and can become quite a pissing contest as to which motor is better. It's mostly a *guy* thing so I'll summarize the main things a guy needs to know about diesel motors. First, the only thing a diesel motor needs to run, is air and fuel. If it doesn't run, then it is failing to get one or the other or both. It does not need electricity, or carburetion, or any of that stuff a gasoline engine needs; only air and fuel. What's more, the fuel can be some variation of crude oil, such as home heating oil, kerosene, or number two diesel fuel.

In summary, the modern motor coach is a self contained dwelling system and it's time away from all civilization is limited by it's holding capacity, battery capacity and fuel on board. Other, more intangible limits, might be those of the inhabitants thereof.

Sources

Where do you get motor coaches? How much do they cost? What does it cost to operate them? All logical questions to the new-comer. Not so logical to the old-timer. The old-timer knows all the answers and can come up with some for which there are no questions.

There are four principle sources for a motor coach:

1) Dealers
2) Private Parties
3) Conversion Companies
4) Build-it-yourself

Dealers

Dealers abound through-out our nation. You can expect to be dazzled by their products and their prices. New coaches look so beautiful and attractive. Each one looks better than the last. Financing is available for new coaches from the dealer's lots. Often this financing is such that it extends for 10, 15, or even 20 years, thus making the payments so small, it is little burden for the buyer. Of course, when the vehicle depreciates faster than the loan is amortized, the buyer begins to scratch his head. But, look at all the fun and luxury to which he was exposed.

Virtually all appliances and equipment on a new coach are warranted against failure for the first year or so. I have friends who have had major replacements such as holding tanks, heaters and refrigerators at no cost to themselves except the annoyance of the time lost being in the shop. Most dealers will bend over backwards to please their customers. Not just for the high profit margin they enjoyed but the fact that a pleased customer sends more customers their way and if they develop a reputation for treating their customer with courtesy and consideration, their business will grow.

Private Parties

Caveat Emptor. Buyer beware. This is a good thing to remember when dealing with a private party. Most private sellers guarantee their coach as far as the street. That is, as you are driving off thier property, when you reach the public streets, it's all yours! Some states have laws protecting the buyer against un-disclosed defects. However, remedies take time, energy and aggravation to implement. When buying a used motor coach expect to find some defects. Negotiate your purchase price so you might compensate for minor defects or repairs. Check with some RV maintenance firms and get an estimate for repairing a refrigerator, or an ice maker or replacing a roof air conditioner. Build these contingencies into your

oday. Visit our website http://www.guaranty.com. 00-825-2333. (VIN01859)

ENTAL - 4090 garaged non-smoker, 300 Allison, Pac brake, dishwasher, jacks, awnings, washer/dryer, Gaggenau stove, refrig, 2 TV, VCR, leather seats & couch, e. $140,000 like new. 209-223-4243 CA.

NTINENTAL 37' - Prestige, diesel pusher Cummins, all options, excellent condition. Can send video. Holiday Rambler dealer. We Vs, ag. Ind. Eq & trucks on trade. Minot very, Minot, N. Dak, 701-839-8878 or 800-735- (VIN)

CONTINENTAL 40' - new 1996 paint/graphics te/blue/silver), Cummins 300hp, Allison 6-spd, Pac ke, grey leather furniture, mirror walls, ceramic tile ors, no smoking/no pets. Will trade, no dealers. See August FMCA Rally. $118,000. 713-899-4596 (cell). VIN01492)

1993 CONTINENTAL - 3730 washer/dryer, dishwasher, & lots more on this wide body. A steal at $96,700. Destinations RV, Coburg & Bend, Oregon, 1-888-RV LIVES. (VIN01380)

CLOSEOUT - new 1998 Continental Panther 4006 slideout, 425 Cat, satellite system, washer & dryer, awning & more. Call Mike Phillips 800-825- RV Center, America's largest RV dealer. Email: mikep@guaranty.com.

system, washer/dryer, 300hp 2000 watt inverter. Guaranty specs and video today. Visit our website luxury coaches: http://www.guaranty.com. Guaranty RV Centers 1-800-825-2333. (VIN01712)

1994 IVORY 38' - original owner, 300 Cummins, brake, Allison 6-sp, Safe-T-Plus, jacks, full aw package, 25K miles, excel cond inside, 2TV, q bed, washer/dryer, leather seats-all. Call for extras. $106,000. Stu/Susan 541-479-3691 OR.

1993 IVORY 36' - 300hp Cummins, Pac brake er, washer/dryer, solar panels, 2 TVs, VCR, dish, separate icemaker, microwave/convectio stored, a wonderful coach. 36,000 mi, pvt pa 941-283-9394 FL. (VIN01273)

1992 IVORY 36' - 250 Cummins, mural, w dishwasher, icemaker, new tires & batteries excellent condition. $88,500. 314-44 (VIN01061)

CUMMINS OWNERS, WANT MORE See our add under "Motorhome Par Performance 800-752-5991.

KALAHARI

1994 KALAHARI 34' - warrant Cummins, CD/player, washer/dryer inverter, solar, smoke/pet free. C corvette or hot rod, excellent co 801-278-3358. (VIN)

offering price. Learn what a set of tires will cost. Check on a new paint job. All of these cost items are negotiable during the dicker-ing stage. Also learn what it would cost to add insurance to your requirements. A buy-ers check list for a used motor coach can be found in the appendix.

Conversion Companies

What are conversion companies? These are fabricators who will build a motor coach from a bus shell. Furthermore, they will design a floor plan to please the owner and will include what ever appliances and equipment the owner wishes. In other words, they will produce a custom conversion to the owner's specifications. The approach is the owner has purchased a used bus shell and has a pretty good idea of how he would like it laid out. The owner then contacts one or more conversion companies and requests bids. The procedure is similar to hiring a building contractor to erect a house. A price is agreed upon and normally a 20 percent non-refundable deposit is made. Then as the project proceeds, the owner has changesand the charges escalate and by the time the coach is finished, the owner has spent about double his original budget. On average you can expect to spend in the $100,000 neighborhood plus the cost of your shell.

Another form of conversion company is one which will only convert new shells. These firms will generally have an assembly line and build on speculation. Normally their speculation will be a small percentage of their line since a buyer will select a coach in progress and have it customized as they wish. Motor coaches in this category will range from the high $400k upwards to over $1 million.

But, if you want it done *your way*, this is a great approach to owning a motor coach of your dreams. A list of conversion companies is included in the appendix.

Build-it-yourself

Since there are far more talented people with mechanicals skills than there are millionaires, self conversion is gaining in popularity. This is where a person buys a bus shell, whether it is a city transit type (RTS) or a highway bus such as a Grey-

hound, and converts it to a motorhome. One caution I would like to make: even though the school bus shell is cheap, avoid this form of shell since it is extremely difficult to obtain any form of insurance. Apparently the school bus shell has a stigma attached as a result of the *hippie* bus of the 60s.

City transits, the RTS, are the most inexpensive shell available for do-it-yourself conversions. The principle drawback to this vehicle is the lack of underfloor baggage space for utilities. They have one other disadvantage in that they are designed and geared for city driving and are generally a little pokey on the highways. This defect is easily corrected by adjusting the governor on the engine. More and more RTSs are set up to serve the suburbs, hence they perform on the highways as satisfactorily as an intercity coach.

The favorite shells for self conversion specialist (my name for a do-it-yourselfer), are the GMC 4xxx series, the Silver Eagle, the MCIs and the Neoplans. I have omitted the Prevost since it is the favorite of the megabuck (have-it-done) owner. In addition, I have left out other coaches such as the Brill and the Mack and a dozen others since they are not as popular as those mentioned.

The self conversion specialist can expect to buy a shell for from $5,000 to $25,000. The cost of conversion can range from $20,000 on the low side to over $100k, depending on the equipment and the amount of work hired to be done by others. For those of you thinking of doing such a thing, *The Bus Converter's Bible* by this author gives a pretty good set of instructions how to do it and gives a preview of what you are getting into.

FREQUENTLY ASKED QUESTIONS

In this chapter we try to answer some of the more commonly asked questions concerning the RV lifestyle. Most of the answers are drawn from personal experience. This does not mean the answers given are the last word, only an opinion.

How much are camping fees?

Many RV parks will charge from$15 to $40 plus local sales tax, or bed tax as some city councils call it. Often cable TV will be included at no extra charge. Many now have telephone jacks at each campsite. Other RV parks will have a rate depending on whether you wish to run your air conditioners. Others will charge extra for pets.

Other camping locations are local, regional, state and federal parks. Most of these government sponsored parks are reasonable in their camping fees. Most will charge in the range of $8 to $12 per night. If electricity is available expect to pay slightly more. For those of you over 55, a Golden Age passport is free from the National Parks. This passport allows you to camp in any National park at half the normal rate.

Can you park a 45 foot coach anywhere?

Many of the modern RV parks can accept a 45 foot coach and many of them have *pull-throughs*. This is a camp site where you simply drive into the site and park, and you may then continue through in the same direction when leaving. A lot of the RV parks are designed to accept the new and larger fifth wheel trailer which almost necessitate a pull through site. Many state parks limit the size of the rig to as small as 26 feet. The reason for this is the parks were designed when the principle type of camping was the use of a tent. They will accept campers on pickup trucks and small motor coaches. When planning a trip, it is a good idea to decide where you wish to stop and check the facilities available. Later in this book is an article concerned with over night stopping places.

Can you get TV anywhere?

No. If your rig has a satellite dish the answer is yes. However, with a standard antenna, there are still some locations where TV is impossible to receive. Specifically, if you travel in Mexico and are addicted to TV, a satellite dish is mandatory. In a lot of remote state and national parks, television reception is very poor.

Are there any free sites by the ocean?

Yes there are several locations on the coast where a motor coach may be parked for camping. These are not well known and in some cases, certain restrictions must be met. The military has several beach front camping sites for active or retired members of the service. In some cases, a handicap decal or sticker on your rig will let you park in some harbor parking lots at no charge. And, there are some lonely stretches of beach where RVs just park and no one bothers them.

Where can you dump your holding tanks?

All RV parks have sewer dumps at almost all campsites. If your campsite does not have a dump receptacle, there will be a community dump station elsewhere. Many municipalities will allow dumping at their sewage treatment facility. More and more states are building dump stations at road side rest stops. Finally, virtually any sewer clean-out at any house connected to the sewer will accept the effluent. For those unfamiliar, a sewer clean-out is often located at the side of a house and is a *wye* with a screw-in plug which may be opened to accept the dump hose. Also, if you have a macerating pump on your rig, a garden hose may be attached and you may dump into any toilet your hose will reach.

What kind of fuel economy can one expect?

This depends on the size of your rig and your driving habits. I have had a 24 foot, 4 ton, gasoline powered motor coach and a forty foot, 20 ton diesel powered bus conversion towing a 2 ton car and gotten about seven miles to the gallon in both cases. Furthermore, when I could exert the patience to maintain between 50 and 55 miles per hour, my fuel economy went up to nearly 10 miles to the gallon. Once, between Reno and Sacramento, we got 12 mpg doing over 65 mph. We were going downhill with the wind at our back. On the other hand, a head wind will cost up to 3 or 4 mpg and a long up hill grade will yield only about 4 to 5 mpg. And, in addition, one cannot expect to romp up a hill in a large motor coach as one would in a sports car. Patience is demanded.

The variables affecting fuel economy are: weight, size, wind conditions, motor type, road condition, grade and patience. My patience is limited so my personal fuel economy is determined by the ragged edge of an unlawful speed. My coach just seems to naturally travel at about 70 mph, hence, I get about 6½ miles to the gallon.

How much do tires cost?

Most of us think of tires as consumable items only one level removed from fuel and oil. Plus, tires are probably the single thing on our coach most exposed to wear, tear and danger. We are all familiar with the cost of simple automobile tires, so the cost spectrum begins there and ranges up to about $450 per tire for a passenger bus tire. The average high quality bus tire is about $300 each. One of the tricks is to substitute a big rig truck tire for a bus tire, thus saving approximately $150 per tire. Also, most big rig tires will average between 80,000 and 100,000 mile of service. Therefore, it is probably more appropriate to revise the question to: how much do tires cost per year. If we assume the average motor coach travels about 5,000 miles per year, then the cost per tire-year is only about $15. One other comment is in order. Often the tread on an RV tire will outlast the sidewalls due to the ozone and the sun's UV rays. Tire covers are a good idea to protect your tires from these elements while parked.

Is it necessary to carry a spare tire?

Many people believe it is unnecessary to carry a spare tire since all motor coaches have dual wheels on at least one axle. The theory is to move one of the dual tires to the damaged location and cautiously drive to a repair station. The theory is good, and it will work, but I carry a spare anyhow. Once I was traveling in Mexico with a friend and he damaged a tire on his coach and borrowed my spare. Tubeless tires are extremely rare in Mexico and he couldn't find a replacement, even in Guadalajara, so 6,000 miles later when we got home he returned my spare. This is a matter of personal risk and choice.

Is there a way to get your mail while traveling?

Mail forwarding is a common practice. Family Motor Coaching Association offers this as one of the benefits of membership. The mail is sent to their address in Cincinnati and periodically it is forwarded to the place you specify. In addition there are companies who provide this service.

Can you get E-mail while on the road?

If you want to receive e-mail while away on a trip, use a nationally recognized e-mail address. You may then get your e-mail by logging on to your provider at libraries, and some coffee houses. If you wish you may sign up for free e-mail service at Hotmail.com and Juno.com. America On Line is the most popular ISP (Internet Service Provider) and has toll free phones all over the country. If you have a laptop computer with a modem and a cell phone, you may log on while in the comfort of your own coach.

What are the rules for towing a car?

This subject will be discussed in detail in a chapter on towing. However, while driving, keep in mind you are subject to the same rules as a trailer. For example, always travel in the outside lane except when passing and never, ever travel in the number one or two lanes when on a four lane highway. Always remember to confine your position to the outside two lanes of any highway and the outermost lane unless passing. Also, your speed limit is the same as that for big rig semi trucks.

Are there any places it is safe to spend the night except RV parks?

Yes, see the chapter on en route parking.

What about driving at night?

Night driving is discouraged except in an emergency. Remember you are operating a large vehicle with big overhangs on the front, rear and sides. Also, most of us are getting a little *long in the tooth*, (or we couldn't afford to take the time and expense to enjoy this activity) and our vision isn't what it was when we were young. Keep in mind we are in a self contained comfort station and we are seldom in a position where we must meet a deadline. Don't drive at night. We have the hazzards of animals on the road, rock overhangs and precipitous, soft shoulders. When it gets dark, find a place to park. We have even stopped at a small town police station and let them know our intentions to park in an empty lot in town. If this wasn't acceptable with them, they would tell us where to go.

Should we carry a weapon?

This a personal preference. My personal preference is not to carry a weapon. Too often a weapon ends up being used on the owner. The large motor coaches of today are rather intimidating vehicles and are in a similar category of an unknown factor to a thief. Common sense should be used when choosing a place to camp or to simply spend the night In over 20 years we have never needed the protection of a weapon and have traveled extensively in Mexico and the USA. If you try to enter Canada with a weapon, it will be either confiscated or sealed until you return to the US. Canada will allow shotguns to enter if it is obvious they are used for hunting. Riot guns, however, are taboo. If you carry a weapon into Mexico, it will be confiscated and you may be arrested.

Is Roadside Service Insurance worth it?

This is a service which will provide simple mechanical repairs on the road or tow your coach if necessary. Although I have never used this service, I have many friends who have and it is cheap enough. I recommend it.

Where do you learn about campgrounds?

There are several directories of campgrounds. *Woodalls* is the most popular. It lists every campground in the country and many in Mexico and Canada. We did have an experience where the only two campgrounds in a small Mexican town were out of business when we got there. This was a case where we asked the local police where they would recommend we park for the night and were directed to a city park. The Elks Lodge has a directory for members. Government publications list the national parks and many road maps will identify regional parks. Software such as Street Atlas USA also lists parks and attractions.

Are there RV clubs we can join?

Family Motor Coach Association and Good Sam are two national organizations which have active local chapters. FMCA (Family Motor Coaching Association) sponsors two national conventions each year. In addition, it is an umbrella for several hundred chapters for those with special interests such as a local area, a make of motor coaches or an activity. In addition to the national conventions, each chapter will have a number of rallies each year for their members and each region will sponsor an annual rally. See the chapter on associations for more detail.

Isn't propane gas dangerous?

A properly designed propane system is as safe in a motor coach as natural gas is in your home. People who have grown up with natural gas regard it as safe, clean and efficient. However, those who have only lived with coal or heating oil tend to be afraid of propane and will only trust electricity. Back East, any vehicle with propane on board is not permitted to use the tunnels, since the authorities are concerned an accident would be disastrous.

Any questions we have left out will be answered elsewhere in this book

RV Insurance:
ARE YOU MANAGING YOUR COVERAGE?
John C. Miller

Why do RV owners buy insurance? To satisfy legal requirements - absolutely. For ethical and moral reasons, that is, to do the right thing in case of a future problem - certainly. Arrange for protection - yes, yes, yes! All other concerns, even legal, are overcome in our minds by the urgency of protecting our investment in that new piece of rolling stock sitting in the driveway. Regardless of your personal financial situation, insurance is where you start.

If that is the case, why don't more RV owners manage their insurance portfolios? In my experience of giving scores of insurance seminars to RV owners around the United States, there is a woeful lack of knowledge about their coverage.

Some have too many cards in their personal insurance deck but most have too few or the wrong ones.

Getting To Where You Should Be

If you will stay with me for a few paragraphs, I am going to give you some helpful hints on getting to where you should be with your insurance coverage and staying there. As I just suggested, managing your insurance is your responsibility, not the insurance company's, nor your agent's, even if he is your good buddy.

For starters, you need to know the right questions to ask. Some, not all, of the information important to your awareness of your coverage is printed on the policy.

What happens if you should have a chargeable accident- -the very reason you want protection? One important fact is not printed on your policy, but it is a fact needed to make management decisions.

A Chargeable Accident And Surcharges

Few RV owners are aware that when you report a chargeable accident against your policy, you will be subject to a surcharge at your next policy expiration. Depending on the company, it will add 25 to 50% to your current premium for each of the next THREE years. If your company charges 50%, that quickly could cost you a lot of money. But only if you have a chargeable accident.

But a more immediate reason you need to know about the surcharge level of your company is to calculate the added cost of reporting the accident to your insurance company. . . not to be confused with the dollar level of the legal requirement for reporting an accident to your state.

For example, assume the cost of the accident repairs are $1,500 and your annual insurance premium is $1,000 with a $500 deductible. The surcharge would be $500 so would you break even by reporting? No! Because the surcharge, remember, lasts three years so reporting the accident will actually cost you $500 times three.

You get $1000 after your deductible but the surcharge adds up to $1,500. The bottom line is you would be in the hole by $500 so you might want to consider coughing up the money yourself instead of asking your insurance company to pay.

Liability Limits Are Often Too Low

Other important management decision facts are written on your policy. But you must be in firm control of their meaning. I usually ask my RV audiences what $25,000/$50,000/$10,000 means on their policy and point out that those numbers represent the legal minimum in some states.

If no one has numbers that low on their policy, I say, "excellent," and move up to numbers that are more common for RV owners such as $100,000/$300,000/ $50,000.

The basic question I pose remains the same- -what do these numbers mean? And why do I say excellent if no one has smaller numbers? Do I sound like a greedy insurance agent or someone trying to help you be better managers? It gets back to the protection concern and getting to where you (for your personal situation) should be?

One at a time - the first $100,000 is the amount of bodily injury liability you have purchased in case one person is injured in one accident. If there are multiple injured in one accident, the $300,000 is the amount of your policy's limit for all bodily injuries. The final $50,000 in the string of numbers relates to the amount of dollars you are insured for to cover the property damage. If a new motor home is involved, would $50,000 be enough? Not likely for a total loss!

What if your policy has limits which are too low for the severity (total losses) of the accident? That's also part of your management (protection) concern - knowing your personal assets level and getting to where you should be. If your insurance dollars run out before damages are satisfied, you could still be twisting in the wind, and your own estate in danger.

Higher Liability Limits Not Expensive

And this is the good news portion. Higher limits of liability are relatively inexpensive. Personally, I recommend $500,000 as the basic level of liability and in a slightly modified form called "combined single limit." This simply means that there is $500,000 liability available to cover the entire accident - all personal injuries and property damage (PL and PD).

In one Western State where the legal minimum is 25/50/10 (which I will not personally write for an RV), the jump to 100/300/50 will increase your premiums by only $6.00. And to extend to $500,000 combined single limit liability coverage costs $29.00 more. Here's another chance to make a good management decision and bring your personal coverage up to where you should be.

Over Coverage And Overpaying

How much is your RV insured for if you should have a total loss - say, a collision or a fire? Let's assume it is five years old and you paid $75,000 for it. Are you still paying for a $75,000 unit or have you reduced it to its present "actual cash value" (ACV in insurance lingo) of probably $35,000?

---

*(FULL COVERAGE EXAMPLE - $250 deductible for collision and comprehensive, 100/300/50 PI and PD, 100/300/50 uninsured motorist, $10,000 medical, full service towing).

If you do not do this each year, you are overpaying your premiums and the bad news is this is expensive OVER COVERAGE. For example, declaring $75,000 ACV for a full package coverage* will cost $641 in the same Western State noted above. The full package costs $464 if your insured RV value is $35,000.

And more bad news - if you have a loss, your insurance recovery will be the current ACV, not the amount of your now overstated original value. You have been throwing money into the insurance company's profit barrel and your agent's pocket as well.

Insurance companies (and many agents) don't argue if you are a poor manager and overstate. In fact, that is why some companies will not allow you to change to ACV as your coach depreciates, even though they know you won't get paid the full amount if you have a total loss. Your management responsibility also includes picking the right insurance company that allows you to properly manage.

Full Timers - Many Of You Are Not Covered

Not so long ago in this rapidly burgeon

ing RV insurance world, full timers could not even get coverage (as full timers) so they didn't tell the truth about living in their motor homes year round.

Some full timers are still uncertain because their agent's are not familiar with RV insurance. And many others think they have coverage but do not. It is still a fact of insurance life that there only SEVEN companies which offer complete full timers insurance. If you want to know if your company is one of them, call your agent or your company's home office (use their 800 number).

If they don't offer coverage, and your agent is unable to help you, call my 800 number and I will tell you which companies offer insurance to full timers. Yes, it does cost more, but it beats the alternative--no coverage at all.

Other Management Tools

Now lets talk about deductibles and replacement coverage (guarantees of original purchase price) instead of ACV, in case of loss. Those are two other management tools you should consider in your new proactive role of "Personal Insurance Manager."

Every RV owner should be the personal manager of his insurance coverage. Who cares more than you - certainly not the insurance company nor the policy writer - your agent, even though he or she may be a good friend?

Earlier, I discussed choosing the right level of liability limits, and making good decisions because of a surcharge which will be invoked against you IF you have a serious loss and make a claim for a chargeable accident.

I pointed out that to be a good insurance manager and make sound choices, you must have correct information at hand, which you can get from your policy or by asking the right questions.

New Management Tools For Consideration

Replacement Insurance and Reducing Deductibles are two relatively recent potential money savers you should ask about to further help you get to where you should or want to be.

I venture that very few of you have replacement coverage if your motor home should be a total casualty loss - through accident or fire. Replacement coverage means that you will get a brand new or like kind (as near as possible) RV in the year of your total loss. In reality, there are only a few companies which even offer replacement coverage. Is your company one of them? Maybe.

What most RV owners would get is (today's) actual cash value (ACV) as compensation in the case of a total loss. So if you think your five year old $75,000 motor home is going to be replaced, think again. You will more likely get $35,000. If you haven't been updating (managing) your insurance portfolio, you are probably paying for $75,000 of coverage.

If it is what you want, find out if your company offers true replacement coverage and how much it costs. For obvious reasons, it does cost more. Perhaps it would give you added peace-of-mind.

Here's what one company offers: for motor homes which cost less than $150,000, you buy replacement coverage for an additional premium of $70.00 per year. If your coach or trailer has a brand new value up to $350,000, adding the replacement rider will cost you $138.00 more per year.

MODEL YEAR LIMITS

You can buy the coverage at any time within the first five model years, but it also expires at the end of the fifth model year. And then, for the next five model years, you can buy a modification that guarantees the insured "original purchase value," in the event of a total loss.

The cost for an "original purchase value", guarantee is slightly lower - $60.00 per year for RV's with an ACV under $150,000 and $91.00 for a coach or trailer with an ACV under $350,000. Be aware that if you are the second or third owner, the insurance company would calculate your purchase price, not the brand new cost.

Let me also take a moment to clear up a frequent confusion regarding model years. If we are in the 1994 model year, it must be counted as year one. 1995 would be model year two so the end of the fifth model year for replacement coverage eligibility is actually December, 1998.

Variations From Different Companies

Other insurance companies have variations of replacement coverage. One allows a delayed purchase of a replacement type policy only within the first 13 months of new ownership. It can be extended for only three model years, for example, 1994-1996. And in that third year, the insurance reimbursement becomes optional.

The company can offer you a new coach or ACV plus $25,000. The option could still cost you money if the ACV plus $25,000 falls short of actual replacement, e.g., the ACV is $100,000 but a new model now costs $150,000. And remember, the insurance company elects the option, you don't.

And there are other companies which offer replacement coverage but absolutely require you to make the choice only at the time the coach is brand new. It cannot be purchased later at any price.

And a final footnote - neither replacement nor original purchase value coverage is offered if you have an RV in the top lines $350,000 and higher. These exclusions represent about one percent of the RV population.

Deductibles Offer Good Savings

The ideal insurance policy would replace all losses, no matter the cause, and not cost you a dime. Right? As with our problem of finding and buying replacement coverage (no cost plus improvement), that is seldom the case. So now let's consider the concept of deductibles.

The deductibles idea requires you pay the first $100 or $250, or maybe $1,000 of the accident cost. And of course, the lower the deductible amount bringing greater risk to the insurer, the more premium you pay. Unless you are a lousy driver, and that does not describe most RV owners, I recommend a high deductible. There are some good incentives for making that choice.

I like a package called a reducing deductible. Every year without a claimed loss except towing), your deductible is reduced by 25% (from the starting point). At the end of four years, without paying extra, you have a zero deductible policy, no matter the level you chose to begin with. So with four years of safe driving, you are rewarded by paying the same amount as if you had a high deductible clause. It makes more sense to me to start with a higher deductible if you are a good driver and elect the reducing feature. Another incentive - the reducing deductible is even available at no cost if you buy either the replacement or the original purchase value package.

Many Choices But Worth Your Time

There are many possible selections with insurance and insurance companies. Your time is money if you use it to study the alternatives. You just can't assume that your agent or someone else will do it for you. Yes, it is my ethical responsibility to advise my clients toward the right insurance and best value for the money. Yet it is impossible for me or any agent to know where each insured should be for their personal circumstance - the value of their estate and risk related to potential harm.

Your job, as your own personal insurance manager, is to find out who offers what and for how much. Depreciation is taking at least a 10% hunk of ACV each year so you should be updating your portfolio and stated insurance value at least every two years.

Full Timers

Are you a full timer? As a reader of this particular book, you might be. If so, do your agent and/or your Insurance Company know that you are a Full Timer? Do they even know what Full Timer means?

As an RV Insurance specialist, I can tell you that I get calls from Full Timers every day who are NOT COVERED but will argue heatedly that they are covered.

How can I know from a phone coversation and without even looking at their policy? Because I ask who their insurance carrier is, and if they do not name one of SIX companies, they are not covered with complete insurance as a full timer! (As of this writing, there were only five insurers, another has now jumped in).

Definition Of A Full Timer

A full timer, in our RV world, is someone who uses his motor coach, trailer or 5th wheeler as his primary residence. One of the seven companies which does insure full timers identifies you this way: anyone who lives in the unit five (5) consecutive months a year.

If you are in the above category and you have any doubts about your coverage, call your agent or insurance company. or you can call our hotline (listed at the end of the article), and I will give you the names of the seven companies. No, I do not represent them all.

Well, what is the penalty if your company does not know you are a Full Timer or says you have coverage but is not one of the six which do offer complete Full Timer coverage?

A Loss Is Your Only Worry

The only time you need to worry is if you have a loss. But wait a minute, isn't that why we have insurance - so we don't need to worry? I return again to my theme throughout this chapter - managing your own insurance portfolio.

If your agent tells you that you are covered as a Full Timer and he represents a company other than the seven, ask him to put it in writing, or show you in the policy that Full Timers are covered. Accept nothing less. Verbal assurance is not good enough.

The most common argument I receive

from Full Timers who disbelieve when I tell them they are not covered is, "I've been with (XYZ) company and/or (My Buddy) agent for years and they have always been square with me."

I have stopped arguing with these hardheads because they don't want to be confused with the facts but readers, don't be stupid! Check it out yourself. The seven companies who insure Full Timers offer insurance besides RV coverage, but they do not include the BIGGEST names in the auto insurance business.

For those who wish to continue the delusion, here is what could happen. In case of a major loss, the company can claim misrepresentation, that 'is, they can claim they would not have written the policy had they known a pertinent fact, in this case, that you were a Fulltimer. No payoff because, in their judgment, you were never insured. The best you might get is a refund of the premium.

Misrepresentation is also possible if you do not declare your Fulltime status to any company which offers the added coverage. Full Timers obviously have more exposure to the possibility of an accident or casualty occurrence. Therefore, it shouldn't be surprising that insurance companies charge more for the basic package geared for Full Timers. The good news is that part of the extra charge includes a most important additional insurance protection.

Full Timers Need What Extra?

In past articles we have discussed your role in managing adequate levels of liability, PI and PD (personal injury and property damage) updating depreciating coach values - and options for replacement coverage and/or guaranteed purchase price, and reducing deductibles.

But you know that full timers have extra needs. Part of the extra charge required above adds one more management tool. It is the equivalent of a "homeowners'" clause, which treats your coach or trailer as a house, rather than strictly a "recreational" vehicle.

This coverage gives you liability protection against an accident which might occur in your camp site--inside or outside. As usual, these coverages depend on the amount of Fulltimer liability purchased. Sample range: $62 to $113 annually. The

$62 would buy $50,000/100,000, that is, coverage for one injury up to $50,000 and $100,000 maximum for multiple injuries. For $113, you can get $500,000 worth of protection.

Do you have a full timers' type policy that includes a homeowners' clause? Read your policy or ask your agent You undoubtedly had homeowners' coverage when your home was in a permanent location so a wise choice is to continue at the same level as before. The amount will depend on your personal cirucmstance - size of your estate and potential for exposure. The familiar term "deep pockets" applies here.

Personal Effects And Contents

Most full timers are drastically underinsured on their personal effects and contents. So are most RV owners, in general, but Full Timers are traveling with a larger share' of their worldly goods, so they definitely need more insurance protection.

What we are talking about is "everything loose which did not come with the unit." A partial list: clothing, bedding, golf clubs, tools, computers, cameras, jewelry, bicycles, folding chairs, barbecue, silverware, mats.

Some of these categories have a unit limit. For example, one insurance company places a $500 maximum on each declaration of jewelry, golf clubs and cameras.

For insurance purposes, attachments to the Coach, such as satellite dishes, awnings, and solar panels should be added to the value of the Coach itself, not listed as personal effects. Have you told your agent about these additions?

A recent unfortunate example: our full timer had purchased only $5,000 worth of insurance for his contents but after a fire destroyed his coach, he added up his replacement costs and the bill came to $18,000. He was adequately covered for his unit but came up $13,000 short for his poor management decision regarding "loose items."

How much would it have cost? An extra $6 per thousand. He was paying $30 for $5,000 coverage, he should have had $18,000 at $108 annually.

And here we have another case of managing. As pointed out, RV insurance companies which offer full timer coverage are seven. Those which offer replacement cost insurance for contents reduces down to three. Now you need to find out at least two more things about your insurance company.

BITS AND PIECES

If you need heart surgery, would you pick a general practitioner to do it? If you need to throw a touchdown pass, would you pick a linebacker to make the toss? Then why shouldn't you consider a specialist when you choose your insurance agent as an adviser for your RV insurance? Here are a few recent examples of situations that were solved by our RV insurance specialty agency.

Number #1 - A new RV coach was on order, not to be delivered for several months. The owner had an opportunity to lock in a lower loan interest rate by acting immediately. Even though there was no vehicle on the road nor actual risk, the loan agency insisted on a certificate of insurance.

We wrote the policy but purchased the absolute lowest minimum in each category as required by the insured's particular state law. When the owner takes possession of his coach for actual usage, we will amend the policy, choosing the proper amounts for the insured's circumstance..

Savings - aprroximately $400 plus the enabling of savings on loan interest.

Number #2 - An unusual vehicle was purchased to pull a 5th wheel unit. It is a Freightliner tractor but it is classified as a commercial vehicle rather than a motor home. Insurance rate differential for a commercial unit versus a motor home is a multiple of two-and-a-half. Because of our RV expertise, we were able to convince the Insurance carrier that the towing vehicle should be reclassified as a motor home.
Savings - aprroximately $1,500.

Number #3 - An RV owner parked his brand new (6 months old) unit in a Sun Belt RV park. He readied the unit for an extended absence by turning off the water from the park faucet but opened the valves inside his RV.

A park employee came by and turned on the water. The unit was flooded, including an overflow of the gray and black water holding tanks. Damage estimate was $70,000 on a book valued unit of $160,000 high/$120,000 low.

The insured RV owner had replacement insurance so we were able to negotiate him a brand new coach, rather than opt for repairs. We also convinced the bank to continue the same loan as with his original unit. That saved him an interest rate jump of 1 to 2%.

Savings - not exactly calculable but we sure have a happy customer.

Number #4 - A Fulltimer owns a golf cart which is permanently kept at a Sun Belt RV park. The question was how to insure it for liability during use.

The easy solution was to increase the level of personal property coverage in the Fulltimer's RV Homeowner's clause. However, the insurance is only applicable to the unlicensed golf cart when operated on private property.

Savings - only $25 but this coverage is normally not available for RV's.

Number #5 - A RV onwer called to cancel his policy with a rather vague reason for doing so. Later, he called back and sheepishly admitted he had been led astray by a competitor's quote which he believed to be somewhat lower than our agency's. He soon discovered why it was lower (and then only minimally) - it was for only six months.

We never make RV quotes for six

months - only on an annual basis. If you get a lower quote, make certain all the facts are correct. because when all the facts are equal, we have a 90% plus success ratio in saving money for new clients, and frequently with better coverage.
Savings - $300.

The Miller RV Insurance team is headed by John C. Miller of Lake Oswego, Oregon. His pickup camper has given way to a series of motor coaches called "Miller Time". John travels around the U.S. and Canada in his latest coach and gives insurance seminars to the RV fraternity. For further information call 1-800-622-6347

Editor's note: The other major RV insurance specialist is RV Alliance America, formerly Alexander and Alexander,
phone: 1-800-521-2942

Associations

Sheila Donigan

In the twenty seven years my family and I have been motor homing we have belonged to several associations. We have had the opportunity to travel the United States, Canada and Mexico in our recreational vehicle and have met some of the most interesting people from all walks of life.

To digress a bit, in my 25 years of corporate life I spent many years traveling. Unfortunately, my travels were limited to hotels and motels. What a difference. Nameless faces and lack of communication due to the requirements of a person's livelihood.

Belonging to something with a common bond enriches a person's life immeasurably. Whether it is stamp collecting, antique cars, bird watching or recreational vehicles having a common interest and desire makes living on this planet much more enjoyable.

Fortunately as a motor home owner there are many associations that would be of interest to almost everyone. Probably the largest "association" is the Good Sam Club. This organization is a "for profit" company that invites owners of every type of RV to join. They have conventions, rallies, chapter get-togethers, member benefits and monthly magazines to inform and to educate. Many campgrounds offer discounts to Good Sam members.

Another large association is the Escapees. This group of "full timers" offer many of the same benefits as others as well as a permanent facility for those who are unable to travel.

Retired military are invited to join S.M.A.R.T.. This active association is growing by leaps and bounds. Their gatherings are called "musters" and they have chapters all over the United States.

The association my family and I are most familiar with, is the Family Motor Coach Association. This organization is strictly for motor home owners and families. The almost 400 chapters in the United States meet frequently in every location imaginable. The membership currently is at over 114,000. Many members choose not to belong to a chapter for whatever reason. They enjoy the multiple member benefits, the monthly magazine and the two international conventions held yearly. As a former officer of this organization, I have had the pleasure to meet thousands of people who have enriched my life because of the common bond of owning a motor home.

Many of you have seen advertisements in various publications regarding trade shows and conventions. Whether you own an RV or not you should attend one. Never use the adage “do I need it or do I want it.” Learning about the lifestyle and meeting others who live it, is what it is all about. Motor home people are the most outgoing and friendly people on the face of the earth. Imagine yourself sitting in a hotel or motel room at the end of a day or sitting by a campfire listening to good music or recapping the day with a new friend. I know what my choice would be and I made it.

Your local public library will list the many associations that are available for membership. I urge you to look at all of the information and request information on one or more that interest you. Stop and talk to people at rest stops and fuel stops if you see an identifying emblem that denotes an association. Many have toll free numbers to call for additional data.

If you are looking for fun, fellowship and more knowledge about the lifestyle that you are thinking about or are enjoying, join an association and learn what fun really is about.

National Camping Clubs

Escapees RV Club
100 Rainbow Dr.
Livingston, TX 77351
409-327-8873

Family Campers & RVers
4804 Transit Rd.
Building 2

Depew, NY 14043
716-668-6242

Family Motor Coach Association
(Motorhome owners only)
8291 Clough Pike
Cincinnati, OH 45244
513-474-3622

Loners on Wheels
P.O. Box 1355 Poplar Bluff, MO 63902
573-686-9342

RV Elderhostel
75 Federal Street
Boston, MA 02110-1941

RVing Women
P.O. Box 1940
Apache Junction, AZ 85217
602-983-4678

S*M*A*R*T
Special Military Active Retd. Travel Club Inc.
600 University Office Bld.
Suite 1 A
Pensacola, FL 32504

904-478-1986

The Good Sam Club
2575 Vista Del Mar Dr.
Ventura, CA 93001
805-667-4100

The Int'l Family Recreation Assoc.
P.O. Box 520 Gonzalez, FL 32560
904-477-7992

The National RV Owners Club
P.O. Box 520
Gonzalex, FL 32560
904-477-7992

ESCAPEES

History and Purpose of Escapees

In a monthly column they were writing for *Woodall's RV Travel* magazine, Joe and Kay Peterson agreed to start a club for full-time RVers. Its official birthday was July 4, 1978.

A contest was held to name the club. "Escapees" was suggested by Harry and Peggy Lewis #22, who also suggested the acronym SKPs. Members began calling themselves SKiPs because it was easier to say than Escapees. It has become a commonly used nickname.

Escapees is a club in the dictionary definition: "an organization of persons for fellowship or other common objective."
A 5-page newsletter was mailed in August 1978 to fewer than 100 members. SKPs now publishes an 72-page magazine for over 28,000 active member-families.

The club adopted the logo of a house in a wagon as the Escapees trademark. It is used on all club documents, but more fanciful versions of a house in a wagon may be used by chapters for their individual chapter logos.

The purpose (mission) of Escapees is to provide a support network for RVers by fulfilling the RVer's three basic needs that are explained in the acronym "S-K-P."

Short-term free parking is available at Escapees parks for those who just want a safe place to stop for a few days. Escapees offers free parking and a low-cost full-hookup campground at its headquarters. Escapees was incorporated in January 1986 in Texas and is governed by a board of directors elected by the shareholders

What is an SKP?

SKP was originally used as an abbreviation of Escapees. (Say S-K-P fast and it sounds like Escapees.) Many members began calling themselves SKiPs because it was easier to say. It has become a commonly used nickname.

Escapees (SKPs) are Special Kinds of People who are always ready to help each other, but S-K-P can more accurately be used to designate the three distinct concepts on which the club is built.

S - Stands for Support

One important benefit of Escapees is the support members get from each other as they travel. Because most Escapees travel long distances from their home base and families, and because they may be on the road for many months at a time, it is important to be part of an extended family of travelers. Support also includes the many benefits and optional services that the Escapees Club provides.

K - Stands for Knowledge

Members often say that the money-saving tips they get from *Escapees* magazine alone more than pay their annual dues. Learning is also the keynote of the semiannual Escapades that take place each spring and fall. Going to an Escapade is like attending a concentrated five-day college course on RVing.

P - Stands for Parking

One thing that makes the Escapees Club different from other RV clubs is that it offers members places to park. In addition to home-base benefits for those who **join** a SKP Co-Op or Rainbow Park, **all** Escapees members may use short-term parking at Escapees parks. This includes Rainbow's End campground, located at the international headquarters in Livingston, Texas. Members also have overnight parking opportunities with other Escapees members across the country.

FAMILY MOTOR COACH ASSOCIATION

THE FAMILY MOTOR COACH ASSOCIATION (FMCA) is an international organization for families who own and enjoy the recreational use of motorhomes. Some of these members live in their motorhome on a full- or part-time basis. A portion of the membership is from the commercial recreational vehicle industry: dealers, manufacturers, and RV component suppliers. The Association is owned by its membership, governed by elected officers, and has a paid staff of employees working from its national headquarters in Cincinnati, Ohio. The Association operates under a non-profit charter.

FMCA WAS FOUNDED IN 1963 in Hinckley, Maine, by a contingent of "house car" owners. A monument to commemorate the founding of the association was dedicated at the Good Will-Hinckley School, site of the founding meeting, on July 4, 1994. The purpose of the Association is to organize social activities, exchange valuable motor coach information, and supply numerous benefits made possible, in part, by collective purchasing. The interest of the Association also extends into the area of political and legislative action, supporting recreational programs and the legal rights of RV owners.

WHILE FMCA takes pride in the merit of its numerous benefits, foremost, and irreplaceable, is the camaraderie and friendship gained from people enjoying the common interest of motor coach travel and recreation. The Association is rich in the tradition of FMCA members extending hands of genuine friendship to one another.

FMCA MEMBER BENEFITS

Membership in FMCA brings with it a wealth of benefits designed to enhance the motorhome lifestyle. Below are brief descriptions of some of the many benefits FMCA offers. For more detailed information, please contact our Membership Department at: 1-800-543-3622.

Every member of FMCA receives a subscription to the association's official monthly publication, Family Motor Coaching magazine. FMC brings you the latest information on association activities such as chapter news, rally schedules and committee activities, in addition to travel and entertainment articles, the latest developments in motor coach design, new coach products, technical information, and the best in advertised coaches, products and supplies.

FMCA members can participate in special insurance programs designed to offer the best coverage available on the market today at a minimum cost.

Trip routing service provides maps to help you reach your destination on time, traveling by your choice of most-direct or most-scenic route.

Each member family is issued a pair of numbered identification emblems for attaching to the front and rear of their motor coach. These allow FMCA members to recognize each other on the highway, in addition to letting others know that the coach occupants are abiding by the association's Code of Ethics.

Accidental death insurance coverage is au tomatically extended to all FMCA family members.

Family Motor Coaching magazine features the Motor Coach Mart, an exclusive classified listing of motor coaches and coach equipment. Rates are economical, AND as a member, you may place a FREE 20-word classified ad once per year, (ONE ISSUE ONLY).

FMCA members who encounter any type of emergency prohibiting them from driving their coach while away from home may be assisted by a member volunteer "pinch-hit driver" who will transport the motorhome to the desired destination of the owner, at the owner's expense.

Typical gathering of coaches at a national FMCA convention

FMCA provides a message service to assist traveling members.

Members are encouraged to visit and participate in the activities of the organized chapters of FMCA. Over 385 chapters provide year 'round rallies for fun, fellowship and entertainment.

The FMCA Membership Directory is designed to help members identify each other in their travels. There is also a listing of members volunteering emergency assistance to other members who experience trouble on the road. This book is one of the most useful and popular benefits of membership. RV Alliance America (formerly Alexander & Alexander), Progressive Insurance, Royal Insurance and the Family Motor Coach Association have cooperated in developing a system to discourage the theft of members' motor coaches and established a reward "for information leading to the arrest and conviction of persons burglarizing a member's motor coach." This includes burglary to the coach as well as total theft of the vehicle. Other companies that provide this service are listed under the insurance heading of the Business Service Director section of Family Motor Coaching magazine.

FMCA has an expanding program of discounts that include savings at some campgrounds across the country, on motor coach components and accessories, and on car rentals. Many of these discounts are listed in the annual FMCA Membership Directory; others appear in the magazine or are announced through membership mailings.

FMCA has chosen Ganis Credit Corporation, one of America's largest RV lenders, to provide a nationwide motor coach finance program that is exclusive to FMCA members.

By enrolling in a special program, FMCA members can have the security of knowing that their medical transportation needs will be met with the speed of modern air transportation.

FMCA Members from across the country and abroad gather to view exhibits of coaches and the latest in accessories and components, attend valuable seminars, enjoy entertainment, meet old friends and make new ones.

FMCA has nine geographical areas and one international area. In addition to the FMC international conventions, FMCA members can attend rallies hosted by FMCA's areas throughout the year. Join the fun and fellowship of these area rallies and take part in their seminars, entertainment and exhibits.

FMCA's Teenage Travelers (TATS) is an organized group of young people who schedule their own activities to have fun during FMCA international conventions. FMCA's annual Membership Directory features a section called "Stoppin' Spots,"

which lists members who have volunteered their home facilities to fellow members for a 24-hour emergency stop. Some of these volunteers have also offered to help find mechanical assistance or have offered their homes as stop-over spots on a 24-hour friendship visit basis. No other RV organization can offer this valuable service.
If you have a heavy traveling schedule and have difficulty receiving your mail along the way, let FMCA help with its mail forwarding service.

The VISA card program offered to FMCA members features high lines of credit, an array of special services, and no annual fee.

The Lens Express full-service program (including discounts on eye exams and ordering of frames, glasses and contact lenses) is offered to FMCA members at a special price of $15 per person and $7.50 per dependent for a three-year membership. Those wishing to order only contact lenses receive a FREE one-year membership.

Worldwide Assistance Services provides FMCA members full travel services including reservations for: airlines, hotels, rental cars, rail travel, tour packages, cruises, etc. For airline tickets, WA guarantees that members will receive the lowest applicable published rates at the time of booking, or the FMCA member will receive "Double the Difference" refunded to them. Tickets will be forwarded anywhere in the world, overnight if necessary, at no additional charge.

The Exit Authority lists all businesses and services at every interstate exit and is available to FMCA members at a discounted rate.

FMCA's "Deductible Reimbursement Insurance Plan" is designed to coordinate with member's Medicare or major medical policy and offers financial protection against deductible and coin-insurance out-of-pocket costs when such expenses are incurred at least 50 miles from home.

FMCA's Emergency Road Service & Technical Referral Plan is offered exclusively to FMCA members at a group rate. This comprehensive, 24-hour-a-day roadside program, is supported by chassis and RV technicians and provides access to more than 20,000 contracted service providers throughout the U.S. and Canada.

New FMCA members are sent Flying

J Real Value Cards. The holder receives a discount of 1 cent per gallon of gas or diesel fuel (with a minimum 20-gallon purchase) and/or 5 cents per gallon of propane at any Flying J Travel Plaza or Fuel Stop location when the card is presented at the time of sale.

FMCA Members traveling to Eastern Canada or New England can order an Irving Oil Card to receive discounts on gasoline, diesel, and motor oil purchases.
This program, administered by Seabury & Smith, is designed to help members supplement their personal life and health insurance portfolio. A total of nine insurance plans are scheduled to be offered along with a prescription drug card.

This card, available to members through an arrangement with the American Telecom Network (ATN) and TTI National, a wholly owned subsidiary of Worldcom, offers a flat rate of 14.9 cents per minute 24 hours per day with no surcharges for calls anywhere in the U.S. Use these specially priced cards to exchange addresses and telephone numbers with people you meet while traveling, and at the same time, identify yourself as a member of the greatest motorhome owners organization in the world!

Key tags with the FMCA logo are available for purchase through Kiley Mold company; an order form appears in FMC magazine. Members should call the National Office to identify lost keys; return postage is guaranteed by FMCA.

One of the greatest benefits of FMCA membership is the opportunity it provides for you to enjoy the fellowship of friends from all over who share a common interest.

GOOD SAM

BENEFITS OF MEMBERSHIP IN THE GOOD SAM CLUB:

FREE Subscription to *HIGHWAYS*

10% discount on overnight camping at more than 1,600 RV parks and campgrounds in the United States and Canada

10% savings on RV parts and accessories at more than 1,000 service centers10% discount on LP gas

Mail forwarding

Discounts on Campground Directory and RV and travel publications

Discounts on long distance telephone

service

Discounts on car rentals

Good Sam VIP Auto and RV insurance with average annual savings of $298

Eligibility for Good Sam Club Group Health and Accident Insurance Program

Preferred rates for RV financing and refinancing

Good Sam Credit Card with no annual fee (upon approval)

Eligibility for RV Emergency Road Service Plan and CVP Emergency Roadside assistance Plan

FREE Trip Routing Service

Fun-filled Samboree rallies and Caraventures

Local Chapter camp-outs and outings

FREE spouse membership

Discounted Emergency Assistance Program (EA+)

Discounts on eye exams, contact lenses, and eyewear

Editor's Note

Sheila Donigan has been actively RV'ing since the mid sixties. She started out with a shell camper and as the children grew this evolved into a cab-over camper and then into a motor home. She and her husband Paul are currently on their third motor home.

They became members of the Family Motor Coach Association in 1971 and she became active almost immediately as volunteers at chapter rallies and elected to various chapter offices. She was nominated and elected as FMCA National Secretary in 1981 and served for two years. Employment and home duties required her to take a rest from national office and several years later she became active again at the chapter level.

As a member of 14 chapters, she volunteered as rally trailboss for numerous rallies and served in every office at the chapter level. Sheila was nominated and elected again as FMCA National Secretary in 1991 and served in that capacity for four years. She was elected FMCA Senior Vice President in 1995 and served for two years. She is currently active again at the chapter level.

Knowledge - The Lasting Gift

by George D. Myers

I have listed Recreational Vehicle related books and videos I know of by publisher. The prices are the most current I could find. Do check with the publisher before ordering. Shipping and handling of about $5 per order is usually additional. Some publishers give discounts for larger orders for multiple items. Most publishers accept credit card orders and some accept e-mail orders.

Recreational Vehicle Standards

The first two are ABSOLUTE MUST READS if you are going to convert a bus. They are the national safety standards for the RV industry.

America National Standards Institute (ANSI) (212) 642-4900

ANSI A119.2 - NFPA 501C Recreational Vehicles, 1996 Edition. Standards for the RV industry on all matters concerning safety relating to LP, water, sewage, flammability, safety equipment, and fuel lines. $35+5 S&H= $40

National Fire Protection Association, Batterymarch Park, Quincy, MA 02269 800-344-3555

The "National Electrical Code 1996" is the standard for almost all wiring in the United States. Article 551 "Recreational Vehicles and Recreational Vehicle Parks" is the Article of primary interest, but it refers to many other sections. The NEC comes in three versions. The soft covered code itself costs $47.50. For $77.50 you can get the "National Electrical Code HANDBOOK 1996" (Code and explanations). A CD-ROM or floppy disk version for DOS, Windows, or Mac for $99.50. The Code and the Handbook are available in most large book stores and most public libraries. I expect there will be a new issue early in 1999, as it has been up dated every three years for some time.

Bus Conversion Books and Videos

Epic Conversion Support, P.O. Box 113, Alpha, OH 45301-0113. Internet74023.2223@CompuServe.com. (937) 426-9850. A synopsis of several Epic products can be seen at http://www.busnut.com/articles.htm. Order form is located at http://www.busnut.com/seecs.htm"

Designing Electrical Layouts for Coach Conversions" by George D. Myers, 280 pages of information on coach electrical systems including Power sources, 120 Volt wiring, 12 Volt, 24 Volt, Electrical Appliances, TV Distribution, Sound, CB, GPS, Alarm Systems, etc. This book is designed to give the reader the information necessary to make the many decisions regarding the electrical systems in a conversion. It includes most of the information that has appeared in the "Electrical Shorts" column, plus considerably more. $39.50

Low Cost Conversions by George D.

Myers, A reality check for the conversion hobbyist wishing to build a conversion for under $50,000. It stresses how to avoid the many expensive pitfalls other people building their own conversions have fallen into. $5.00

Fiberglass on Plywood Tanks, By George D. Myers. Detailed description of one way to build good solid economical tanks for water and holding, to the exact size you need. $6.00

Satellite TV by George D. Myers. Information for anyone considering buying one. What you need to know before you buy one. $4.00<> "Super Insulation the Roof" by George D. Myers. Describes a high quality insulation system that can be installed on completed conversions. An alternate approach that gives better insulation while not reducing interior head room. $2.50

Air Brakes / Air Systems by George D. Myers. A very detailed description of coach air brake systems. Includes information on the other systems that use air pressure. The information here could save your life if you don't know how to maintain your air brakes. It could also save many dollars in repairs. $7.00

Coaching With Kids by Anna L. Bakies. How to manage, entertain, and educate children while traveling in a converted coach. It gives many activities to do while on the road and in camp. However, the main point is how to plan that part of the trip involving the children to ensure everyone will have a good time. This Note is especially valuable for grandparents who are introducing their grandchildren to coaching. While aimed at coach travel, the ideas presented in this Note are extremely helpful for any trip that will involve children, whether it is by coach, car, train, or air. $5.00

Raising the Roof (1 hr. 12 min video) by George D. Myers. Covers how he prepared the coach, supported the roof while it was raised, cut the vertical supports, raised the roof, and filled the gaps. $15.00

Bonding Steel Over Window Openings, 1 hr. 45 min. Video) by George D. Myers. Shows how he covered them with 18 gauge steel using Sikaflex to bond it in place. This includes lifting and stretching the steel and installing new RV windows. $15.00

Making a New Front Cap (1 hr. 33

min. Video) by George D. Myers. Shows the fiberglass on plywood method he used to build a redesigned cap for his Phantom. It starts with a large opening and ends with a finished cap. $15.00

Winlock Galey, 26135 Murrieta Rd., Sun City, CA, (800) 205-8254,(909) 943-4945, http://www.winlock.com/,http://bookzone.com/bookzone/indexed/10000526.html,http://www.busnut.com/sewg.htm, and http://www.busnut.com/conv101.htm

The Bus Converters Bible by Dave Galey. How to plan and create your own luxury Motorhome. Provides a description of the various systems in a conversion and gives information on how to lay out the interior. $39.95

The Joys of Busing by Dave Galey. A humorous look at the problems and daily situations that occur while traveling in a bus conversions. Includes technical information on how to solve many of the problems Dave has encountered in his travels. $9.95

The Gospel of Gauges According to Galey by Dave Galey. This book is not only the best I have seen on this important subject, it is the only one. Covers all the instrumentation needed for a conversion including, why each is needed and what it will tell you about your systems. $9.95

Classy Cabinets for Converted Coaches by Dave Galey. There are a lot of books on cabinetry, but this one relates them to conversions. $14.95

Fascinating Fastener Facts by Dave Galey. Includes The Book of Rivet Revelations and a Smattering of Nonsense. There are a myriad of fastening devices and adhesives that are used widely in industry. The technological advances in bonding applications have created many viable, perfectly sound choices available to the do-it-yourself bus converter. 120 pages. $14.95

Slideout Rooms, Mechanics & Structures by Dave Galey. This is a comb-bound book of 96 pages describing the various slide-out room options. It is heavy on structural theory, (possible dull) but has many pictures to look at. The book also discusses sealing, latching and electrical layout. $19.95

Replacement Electrical Control Panel - Includes Parts, Layout, and

Diagrams" by Dave Galey. Developed for those bus owners wishing to up date their bus electrical system, pictures, diagrams, parts list and detailed instructions are provided. All parts are commonly available at your local Auto Parts Store $19.95

Eagle Planning Sheets by Dave Galey. This kit includes (1) right and left outboard profiles, (2) right and left inboard profiles, (3) main and baggage floor plans, (4) cross sections, and a set of typical furniture and appliances drawn to 1/4 inch to the foot scale PLUS several sets of representative floor plans. $19.95

Thomas Interiors, 1361 Bennett Ave. Long Beach, CA 90804-3018, (562)494-4723

The Bus Designer Kit by Thomas Winterhalter. Shows how to design and layout your floor plan and how to transfer that plan to your bus. Includes a double sided laminated grid to develop your layout, seven markers, examples, and instructional documentation.

MAK Publishing, 3431 Cherry Ave. Long Beach, CA 90807 (562) 492-9394

Bus Conversions From the Inside Out by Michael A. Kadletz. Eighteen chapters covering the step-by-step process for turning a bus into the Ultimate Motorhome. $30

MCI-8 (2 hr. Video) by ProBus. Goes over the various systems of an MC-8. $25

Exterior Tape of Commonly Seen Conversion Buses (2 hr. Video) by ProBus. Shows different highway coaches commonly converted to motor homes. $25

Interior Tape of Six Conversions (2 hr. Video) by ProBus. Shows the interior of several conversions giving ideas of layouts furniture etc. $25

Green Publications, 306 Riverbay, Tampa, FL 33619 (813) 621-5296. Free information at P.O.Box 454 Placios, TX 77465

Converting Buses into Motor homes by Bill Lowman. This is a general discussion of the conversion process aimed at the low end owner conversion

Ample Technology, 2442 NW Market St., #43, Seattle WA 98107. Http://www.amplepower.com.

Living on 12 Volts with ample Power" by David Smead (author of Bus Conversion's "Balanced Electrical Systems" column.). This book covers the problems faced by anyone living on the limited 12 volt power whether in a coach, a boat, or remote home. It is intended primarily for the reader who is new to the problems of limited power.

Wiring 12 Volts for Ample Power by David Smead. The rules, standard practices, and available material for 12 volt wiring is different from the 120-VAC wiring many people are familiar with. The book presents general schematics, wiring details, and trouble shooting information not found in other books.

Ample Power Primer by David Smead. Basic information on the electrical concepts and systems needed for a conversion. Excellent section on lead acid batteries. $4.95

F. Marc de Piolenc, P.O. Box 3841, City of Industry, CA, 91744-9991Http://www.sdic.net/piolenc/buscon.htm<>
Conversion Resources - the Bus Conversion Trade Directory compiled by F. Marc de Piolenc. Listing of suppliers for

all the things needed for a conversion. $23.00 postpaid in North America. Bus Book Publishing, Inc. PO Box 9, McMinnville, OR, 97128-0009 -(800) 775- 4577, http://www.busbook.com.

The Bus Pages A Yellow-Pages of bus manufactures, dealers, suppliers, etc. Good source of dealers if you are looking for a shell. Complete listing of all transit authorities if you are looking for local bus auctions. Also lists bus companies by location. $19.95 one time cost for annual subscription.

Recreational Vehicle Magazines

Bus Conversions magazine, MAK Publishing, 3431 Cherry Ave. Long Beach, CA 90807 (562) 492-1345 http://www.busconversions.com Best source for Conversion information. They hold an annual convention each spring. Excellent classified section if you are looking for a shell or completed conversion. Can subscribe by phone or on-line.

Arriving magazine, MAK Publishing, 3431 Cherry Ave. Long Beach, CA 90807 Aimed at high end factory conversions and other luxury transportation

Bus World magazine. MAK Publishing,

3431 Cherry Ave. Long Beach, CA 90807 Targets the seated bus industry.

National Bus Trader magazine, 9698 W. Judson Road, Polo, Illinois 61064. Has good information on buses, including mechanical. Good source of used buses in classified. Annual conversion issue aimed at top of the line conversions. Generally very anti conversion hobbyist and pro factory unit.

Family Motor Coaching The magazine of the Family Motor Coach Association, 8291 Clough Pike, Cincinnati, OH 45244, (800) 543-3622, in OH (513)474-3622. Good source of information on motor home related subjects. Good articles on places to visit. Their Summer and Winter Conventions are affairs to remember. Generally 5-7,000 coaches. Owner built bus conversions were the foundation of the organization, but now it is primarily commercial motor homes. You must own a motor coach to be full member, but an associate membership and a magazine subscription are available.

Motor Home, 2575 Vista Del Mar Dr. Ventura, CA 93001(805) 667-4100. Very anti-owner converted coaches. However, it is a good source of information on accessories and travel articles.

Bus Conversions. Last, but certainly not least, let us not forget a subscription to this magazine, or its sister publications. They are available from MAK Publishing, 3431 Cherry Ave. Long Beach, CA 90807 (562) 492-1345. These include "Bus Conversions" magazine, "Arriving" magazine, and "Bus World" magazine.

To add a post script to this article, if you are hungry for bus conversion information, you really need to get on the Internet. There are three main conversion sites.

http://www.busconversions.com,http://www.busnut.com, and http://www.rv-coach.com. There are other sites for various companies in the field and even one dedicated to RTS conversions.

General RV Books

Available from Amazon.com or local book store.

The RVer's Bible : Everything You Need to Know About Choosing, Using, and Enjoying Your RV - by Kim Baker, Sunny Baker (Contributor) - $19.95 -- 416 pages (April 1997)

Recreational Vehicles : Finding the Best Buy - by Eleanore Wilson (Contributor), Bill, Jr. Alderman - $9.95 -- 123 pages 2nd edition (August 1996)

Living Aboard Your RV : A Guide to the Fulltime Life on Wheels - by Janet Groene, Gordon Groene (Contributor) - $16.95 -- 250 pages 2nd edition (March 1993) <>Cooking Aboard Your RV - by Janet Groene - $13.95 -- 218 pages (March 1993)

Rving Basics - by Bill Moeller (Contributor), Jan Moeller - $14.95 --213 pages (January 1995) King of the Road : A Beginners Guide to RV Travel - by Ted Pollard -$12.95 -- 221 pages (June 1993)

A Guide to Appraising Recreational Vehicle Parks - by Robert S. Saia $19.50 (December 1997)

RV Electrical Systems : A Basic Guide to Troubleshooting, Repair, and Improvement - by Bill Moeller - Jan Moeller (Contributor) - $19.95 (November 1994)

RV Repair & Maintenance Manual - by Bob Livingston (Editor) - $34.95 --400 pages 3rd edition (March 1998)

Managing 12 Volts : How to Upgrade, Operate, and Troubleshoot 12 Volt Electrical Systems - by Harold Barre - $19.95 -- 213 pages (August 1996)

The RV Handbook - by Bill Estes, Bob Livingston (Editor) - $29.95 -- 352 pages 2nd edition (June 1997)

Automotive Electricity and Electronics - by Al Santini $64.95 -- 450 pages 2nd Ed. Edition (July 1992)

Alternative Lifestyle Living and Travel - by Hofmeist, Ron Hofmeister, Rob Hofmeister, Barb Hofmesiter (Contributor) - $12.95 -- 255 revised edition (1996)

How to Buy an RV (And Save Thousands of Dollars) - by Don Wright - $12.95-- 152 pages 2nd Rev edition (April 1996)

Over the Next Hill : RVing Seniors in North America - by Dorothy A. Counts, David R. Counts $16.95 -- 276 pages (September 1996)

RV Having Fun Yet? : Comic Adventures in a Recreation Vehicle - by Ray Parker $12.95 -(October 1994)

RVing for Fun and Profit - by Thomas M. Magee, Tom Magee, Mary Lou Magee $19.95 -(July 1996)

10 Minute Guide to Travel Planning on the Net - by Thomas Pack, Staff Que Development Group - $14.99 -(April 1997)

100 Best Family Resorts in North America : 100 Quality Resorts With Leisure Activities for Children and Adults - (4th Ed) by Janet Tice, Jane Wilford, Becky Danley, Becky Danky (Editor) - $16.95 -- 288 pages 4th edition (January 1998)

Super Family Vacations/Resort and Adventure Guide - by Martha Shirk, Nancy Klepper (Contributor) - $17.00 480 pages, 3rd edition (February 1995)

America's Hidden Treasures : Exploring Our Little-Known National Parks (National Geographic Park Profiles) - $12.95 -- 200 pages Revised edition (April 1997)

The Amusement Park Guide : Fun for the Whole Family at More Than 250 Amusement Parks from Coast to Coast (2nd Ed.) - by Tim O'Brien, Tom O'Brien- $14.95 -- 288 pages 2nd edition (May 1997)

Campground Guides

Trailer Life Campgrounds/RV Parks & Services (annual) - $19.95 - 1700 pages, T.L. Enterprises, 2575 Vista Del Mar Dr., Ventura, CA. 93001-2575 (December of previous year) Lists U.S., Canada, and Mexico, 800-234-3450.

Woodall's North American Campground Directory (annual) - $21.95 (December of previous year) Woodall Publications Corp., 13975 West Polo Trail Drive, Lake Forest, IL, 60045-5000 Available in most book stores and many RV parks. This is the largest campground guide.

Military RV Camping & Rec. Areas Around the World, William Crawford, Sr.Phd. and L. Ann Crawford, Military Living Publications, P.O.Box 2347. Falls Church, VA. 703-237- 0203. Listing of FamCamps open to active duty and retired Military and Civil Service personnel. Wheelers RV Resort & Campground Guide (annual), Print Media Services, Ltd. 1310 Jarvis Ave., Elk Grove Villabe, IL. 60007 800-323-8899 $14.95

Camping with the Corps of Engineers, S.L. Hinkle, Cottage Publications, 24396 Pleasant View Drive, Elkhart, IN., 46517, $13.95, 800-272-5518. The only complete guide to campgrounds operated by the U.S. Army Corps of Engineers.

Don Wright's Guide to Free Campgrounds, Don Wright, Cottage Publications, 24396 Pleasant View Drive, Elkhart, IN., 46517, $16.95, 800-272-5518.

Lists many more low cost than free places. While the copies I have were both published in the same year, this and the Save-A-Buck appear to be essentially identical.

Save-A-Buck Camping, Don Wright, Cottage Publications, 24396 Pleasant View Drive, Elkhart, IN., 46517, $16.95, 800-272-5518, Campgrounds $5 and under. KOA Kampgrounds Directory (annual), KOA Inc., Executive Offices, Billings, MT 59114- 0558, 406-248-7444, available free at their Kampgrounds.

George D. Myers is a well established bus conversion author with two books in print, five short studies called Coach Conversion Notes, three videos, and almost 40 articles in Bus Conversions magazine including his monthly *Electrical Shorts* column.

George started camping at the age of four. He and his new bride bought their first bus in 1971 and converted it. George is a retired Electrical Engineer who brings the engineering analysis and technical writing skills he learned in his professional working days to the bus conversion hobby. He and his wife Sue are FMCA Life Members and have number L2014s.

Getting Underway

After planning a trip and getting ready to go to a rally or convention, it seems like we always forget something. Thus, a check list is really a good idea. And, we need several check lists. First and foremost is the equipment check list. This is equivalent to a pilot walk-around to see everything mechanical is in order. The obvious question I used to ask is, "Will the motor keep running?" One could not tell this from a visual inspection. In our motor coach, however, if the motor stops, it is not fatal and all we have to do is put out a mail box and we are home.

We also need a check list for things we always forget to pack in our suitcase when we go on a trip. These are such simple things we take for granted when we are at home such as, our medication (if any), our address book, and all the every day mundane stuff.

Finally, we need a check list for our *daily camp breaking and trip continuing.* Most may think there is no difference from our *getting ready to go on a trip* list, and our *daily camp breaking* list(dbc). There really is a difference; the *dbc* should be much smaller but might include a few additional items .

The following pages contain several check lists and I consider them *copylefted.* That is, you may make all the copies you wish without infringing on any copyright. I have left a few spare lines where you may insert your own checklist items.

Engine Check List		
	Oil Level	
	Coolant Level	
	Fan Belt Condition & Tightness	
	Battery Cables	
	Battery Water	
	Radiator Hoses	
	Fuel Level	
	Spares	
		Fuel Filters
		Oil Filter
		Belts
		Starter Solenoid

General Coach Check List	
	Tire Condition and Pressure
	Spare Tire Check
	Head Lights
	Marker Lights
	Stop Lights
	Turn Signals
	Tow Ball Hitch & Electrical Socket
	Brake Air Pressure (if applicable)
	Fresh Water Level
	Holding Tanks Empty
	Propane Level (if applicable)
	House Batteries, Water & Cables
	Fresh Water Hose
	Air Hose & Chuck (if applicable)
	Electrical Hook Up Cables
	Electrical Adapters

General Coach Check List (cont.)		
	TV Cables & Adapters	
	Patio Chairs & Tables	
	Awnings Secured	
	TV Antenna (dish) Retracted	
	Dump Hose & Tool Kit	
	Windshield Wiper Blades	
	Electical Adapters	
	Generator Operational Check	
		Oil Pressure
		Water Temperature
		Fuel

Daily De-Campling Check List	
	TV Antenna Down
	Tires Checked
	Oil Checked
	Water Checked
	Lights Checked
	Electrical Disconnected & Stowed
	Holding Tanks Dumped
	Hoses Stowed (water and dump)
	Awning Retacted & Locked
	Pato Furniture Stowed
	Carpets & Mats Stowed
	Step Retracted or Stowed

<table>
<tr><th colspan="3">Inside Coach Check List</th></tr>
<tr><td></td><td colspan="2">Refrigerator On</td></tr>
<tr><td></td><td colspan="2">Pantry Stocked</td></tr>
<tr><td></td><td colspan="2">Ice Maker On</td></tr>
<tr><td></td><td colspan="2">Appliance Operation Check</td></tr>
<tr><td rowspan="4"></td><td></td><td>Microwave Oven</td></tr>
<tr><td></td><td>Cook Top & Oven</td></tr>
<tr><td></td><td>Water Filter Element</td></tr>
<tr><td></td><td>Coffee Maker & Toaster</td></tr>
<tr><td></td><td colspan="2">All Lamps Check & Spare Bulbs</td></tr>
<tr><td></td><td colspan="2">Dishes - Pots & Pans</td></tr>
<tr><td></td><td colspan="2">CB Radio & Stereo Check</td></tr>
<tr><td></td><td colspan="2"></td></tr>
<tr><td></td><td colspan="2"></td></tr>
<tr><td></td><td colspan="2"></td></tr>
</table>

Don't Leave Home Without List	
	Address Book & Phone Numbers
	Books, Games & Cards
	Cell Phone
	Chapter Badges (if appropriate)
	Check Book & Cash
	Clean Underwear
	Clothes, Shoes & Socks
	Daily Medication (if any)
	Drivers License or Identification
	Garage Door & Gate Openers
	House Keys
	Insurance Papers
	Maps and Other Directions
	Organ Donor Card
	Passport (if appropriate)
	Razor & Other Toiletries
	Title to Vehicles

En Route

You have completed all the check lists from the previous chapter and are now ready to go! We will assume you are towing a car. If you are not, play like you are. OK? We are now operating a vehicle slightly larger than a Mazda Miata so your driving habits are going to have to be modified a bit.

Probably the first thing you'll notice is you can't burn rubber. When you leave from a full stop, your feeling of acceleration is more akin to that of a ship leaving the dock. The other major difference is you can't stop on a dime, or even a dollar; more like your pension. Stopping is probably one of the most critical aspects of driving a big rig motor coach. One of my pets peeves is tail-gaiting. If you tail-gait in a motor coach, you are courting disaster. Try to give yourself approximately ten times the spacing in your motor coach that you would in your Miata.

Brakes on your motor coach behave according to your air pressure, and the amount of wear. Slack adjusters should be checked periodically by a professional and should be taken up every 3,000 to 5,000 miles. If you have an air leak your air pressure may fall below the safe level. Another dangerous situation is when in a long line of traffic, i.e., stop and go, your motor is idling and you are applying the brakes often. This uses up your reserve air pressure in your tanks and before you know it, you aren't stopping like you were. It can be very disconcerting!

Be very alert as to your air pressure when in heavy traffic. Furthermore, watch for four-wheelers (another name for cars). Most people driving four-wheelers are oblivious of large vehicles and often swerve in front of them. This is extremely dangerous (for the four-wheeler) since the big-rig stopping distance is probably ten times their stopping distance.

In the old days we used to use the car lengths as a criteria for following distance. Today, it is much more appropriate to use the number of seconds as a following distance. This means instead of using three car lengths for a following distance, you are much safer using three seconds. This is easily determined by observing a marker on the road and counting, one-thousand one, one-thousand two, etc. In a big rig like our motor coaches, we should change this criteria from three seconds to five, or six seconds. Keep in mind momentum is a product of speed and mass. Our speed in our coaches may be the same as in our cars but our mass is probably ten times that of our cars.

The following stories will illustrate what I call **Heart-braking Tales**

I remember one time we were leaving in our first coach to go up north for the summer to get away from the heat. So I decided that it would be a good idea to stop by a mechanic's shop I knew and have the brakes adjusted. This entails taking up on the slack adjusters, a relatively simple job not requiring a great deal of talent, but a need to have just the right touch. Also, you must be willing to get a little dirty.

My mechanic friend was on a service call at the time we got there so I asked his helper if he could do the job. He replied in the affirmative and promptly went under the coach. He fooled around under there for about fifteen minutes for which I gave him a twenty-dollar bill and we were off and on our way.

We were mostly on freeways taking it easy so I didn't have much opportunity to test the brakes, but I was full of confidence. However, as we drove north the brakes didn't seem to be much better and I got the feeling that this mechanic's helper did a number on me. I hated the idea of crawling under the bus and doing what I just paid for, so onward we went.

We had one really nerve shattering incident. While leaving the wine country and proceeding into the redwood portion of Northern California, we ran into some road work with flaggers. You know who I mean, those people who hold up flags and won't let you go on, when it is obvious they are just exercising their awesome power over motorists.

Anyhow, we were just coming around a bend in the road and all of sudden there was a road block, flagger and all! We were doing about 60 miles per hour when Larry in the bus ahead called on the CB that we were stopping. So, in a panic I jammed on the brakes and we did not stop too well. In fact, we were hardly stopping at all! We did slow down and finally came to a rest side by side with Larry's bus, which had presented an obstacle in front of me so I just went around it. Luckily the shoulder was wide enough.

Cautiously, we continued until we got to Eugene, Oregon where we stopped at the Eugene Sand and Gravel maintenance shop. I drove over the pit and asked them to adjust my brakes and lube the coach while there. A few minutes later I was invited to go into the pit to see something they discovered. There was one of my brake cans on the drive axle hanging by an air line that was not attached to the frame. It seems the weld to the framework had broken loose and was no doubt that way when the mechanic's helper back home had been under my bus taking a twenty-dollar nap.

This was in my early days of busing when God takes care of stupid people. As much as I hate to crawl under that cruddy old bus (note: all buses are cruddy underneath regardless of their age, be they fifty years old or just out of the factory), each time we leave on a trip and several times while on a trip, I inspect and tune the slack adjusters.

One other vivid memory of slack slack-adjusters was an experience in Mexico. We had been working our way south down the Baja Peninsula. This "we" was composed of four other bus conversions of various ilks, such as a pair of Eagles, an MC-8, and two GMC 4104s. It was during this trip that the famous *Automatic Wind Compensator* incident occurred. We had spent the night in La Paz and decided to go to Cabo San Lucas via the eastern route. This was a little more mountainous, but much more scenic than the western route, which was much more desert-like.

We had just come out of the mountains and were approaching San Jose del

Cabo when it appeared that my brakes had simply failed. We were coming down a long grade and my Jake brakes didn't seem to hold very well so I started applying my brakes.

There, on the road, a couple hundred yards in front of me, was a small herd of cattle. They were just moseying along without a care in the world, unmindful that nearly 40,000 pounds of machinery was hurtling toward them at 75 miles per hour. Slowly most of them left the roadbed . . . all but one proud bull who, no doubt, knew he owned this road and all the surrounding countryside.

I was last in line in this caravan, so with measured hysteria, I announce over the CB radio,"I'm gonna kill a bull that won't get outta my way and my brakes won't stop me!!" Just as I got to within 15 or 20 feet of this creature, closing at over a 100 feet per second, he swished his tail and calmly, but with indignation, stepped out of my way. I am sure that I missed him by at least an inch and a half.

A mile or two later, I managed to swallow my heart and get my blood pressure down from a tachycardia condition. We traveled a few more miles and pulled over. Under the bus I went with tools and determination to attack those slack adjusters. This was done with a vengeance and we were able to complete the trip without any road-kill.

Over Night Stopping Places

When in route from one place to the next, often it requires several days to complete the journey. Thus we are compelled to find a place to park our rig and spend the night *on the road.*

Obviously, the common choice is the profusion of RV, or trailer parks dotting all the major routes through-out the country. But, what if you do not want to hook-up or even need to hook up while en-route, or are just plain cheap and don't see the need to waste the money on an over night parking place? Still, there is that breed of camper that doesn't feel secure parked outside of a KOA. But, if you are the adventuresome type, and would like to keep a few bucks in your hip pocket, read on!

One of the slickest ways to find free parking en-route is to cultivate a host of friends all over the country and park in the street in front of their house, or their driveway or backyard. If you do this, it is important to insist they throw you a land line so you can hook-up to electricity. Also, if they have a sewer clean out handy, be sure to demand your right to use this as a dump station. This approach may take a couple of years to develop, but I know of a few people who have achieved this remarkable feat.

The simplest place to locate for an over night stay is a regional shopping center. There is almost always one just off the super slab and easy to spot. Many major malls, however, do not allow over night parking and a notice of this fact will be posted. One morning in Ventura, California, we were rousted out at 3:00 a.m. and ordered off the premises by a Rent-A-Cop who informed us of a city ordinance against sleeping in a vehicle. Although this was a blatant self-serving lie, it turned out to be a good thing since we got a jump start toward our home, which was another 100 miles on the other side of L.A. The Ventura Freeway into Los Angeles at that time was under construction and we breezed through between three and four in the morning, whereas the morning rush hour lasted nearly three hours. Since then, when we wish to spend the night in Ventura, we use the J.C.Penney back parking lot.

There are several types of shopping centers that actually welcome RV over-nighters. Foremost among these are the K-Mart stores. It does two significant things for these stores. It increases their parking lot security to have an over-nighter and the next morning they have a potential and grateful customer. It also improves their public image.

Once we entered a regional shopping mall in a large city and noticed a *No Over Night Parking* sign as we came in. So, looking around, we noticed a Sam's Club across the street. We proceeded there and inquired of the manager and learned that almost every night they had two or three RV rigs in their lot. No doubt, a reaction to the snobby mall across the street. He assured us we were welcome. I won't identify the city, but it is located in the southeast corner of South Dakota.

One of the most common over night parking spots is the ordinary rest stop. This is also one of the most disagreeable locations to try to get any sleep. Many rest stops are posted for no over night parking; possibly due to the penchant of some natives for murdering tourists The only place worse than a rest stop for over night parking is a truck stop. The rest stops are unpleasant because of their proximity to the highway and the all night-long-traffic noise. The truck stops are worse because of the large number of trucks with their motors running and their refrigeration generators going, and the incessant din of trucks coming and going all night long. Sometimes, however, you have no choice. I recall one time in a West Texas truck stop. We had looked for a suitable stopping place without success and it was getting late so we couldn't be choosey and had to park in a truck stop. After all, there is safety in numbers. That night the trucks were a minor irritation compared to the *blue norther,* a wind that pounded the coach all night to the degree I felt we may capsize. Little sleep was had that night.

One guaranteed over night parking place is in front of your kid's house. After all, they are family and cannot refuse you. Be prepared, however, to have your electrical hook-ups from the garage to the coach disconnected at any time. This is guaranteed to happen with all the grand-kids, neighbors kids and dogs running around. One time we were in Utah in sub-freezing weather comfortably ensconced in front of one of our children's place. Our electric toe-kick heaters were functioning beautifully along with our propane units. We awoke one morning to discover our pipes in the baggage compartment had frozen, despite a 100 watt bulb burning near our water pump. So the next day we decided to improve our chances by picking up a 1500 watt cube heater from Wal-Mart to keep the baggage compartment nice and cozy. Alas, a kid or a dog kicked our electrical connection loose in the night. This time our pipes froze solid and did not thaw, even by that afternoon. So, we broke camp and headed south. That night we parked in a casino parking lot in Mesquite, Nevada and were awakened the next morning by our water pump continuously evacuating out fresh water through the breaks caused by the freeze.

I could discuss the private camping membership parks but they are normally off the beaten path and are designed more for resort style vacations. They are seldom on the way to your destination and simply do not lend themselves to en-route over night parking.

One of the neatest membership organization is the Elks Club more properly known as the Benevolent and Protective Order of Elks (BPOE). Almost all of the lodges have internal camping clubs and many of the lodges have a mini-camp ground with full or partial hook ups. We have stayed in Elks Lodges' parking lots as humble as a strip shopping center with three business tenants (The Elks being one of them) to several lodges sporting an eighteen hole golf course with 50 amp electrical service. As a visiting Elk, we have always felt welcomed and many locations without camping facilities have run an electrical cord out a window to give us all the comforts we could use. One time, we could not locate an Elk's Lodge in a certain city. We spotted an Eagle's lodge, inquired and learned that the town no longer had an Elk's club. We were, however welcomed to spend the night in their parking lot if we wished. How's that for hospitality?

Another really neat place to park is a marina parking lot. This is especially great if you are a boat lover and aren't most of us? One fabulous location which should be mentioned is Winchester Bay south of

Reedsport on the Oregon coast. There is a fee for parking overnight but this spot has not only the greatest atmosphere but fresh water for your holding tanks and a dump station. One time, by accident, we stumbled upon one of those idyllic locations you dream about. We had pulled off I-90 near Snowquamish in Washington and got lost looking for the small town. Turning down a dirt road we ended up in an isolated area parking next to a running stream with Bald Eagles soaring overhead and total privacy. We have been back a couple times since and it hasn't been spoiled by a developer yet.

Finding an over night spot while en-route is limited only by your imagination and your daring. I hope the ideas contained herein will stimulate your adventuresome spirit.

Mountain Driving

Most of us need no instructions on how to drive or we wouldn't be navigating one of these monsters around. There are, however, some cautions we should be aware of when tooling around the mountains.

There are mountains and then there are *mountains.* Crossing Eisenhower Grade in Colorado is one thing. The winding drive up through Jerome, Arizona is a *whole 'nother experience.*

Perhaps one of the most important tools for mountain driving is the *Jake Brake,* or the PAC brake. These are engine compression brakes for diesel motors. Unlike a gasoline powered engine, which will slow down when you back off the throttle, a diesel engine will not.

A basic rule of mountain driving is: **Which ever gear is used to climb a grade is the gear which should be used while descending**. For example, if you have a ten speed transmission and have to go to eighth gear while ascending a hill, use eighth gear to go down the same degree of grade with your engine compression brakes engaged. This way you will maintain control and will not have a tendency to over speed. Another major advantage of dropping into a lower gear is it will help cool your engine. If you fail to down shift, your brakes could get so hot they may fade or fail altogether. **Never, ever, coast downhill in neutral!** This is a recipe for disaster.

The average motor coach of today ranges between 25,000 and 35,000 pounds. This is approximately 10 to 15 times the weight of an average automobile. Imagine your car going around a curve a little too fast. It is fairly easy to get it back in line. Now imagine your motor coach approach ing a curve a little too fast and you really have a problem. Always drive at a controllable speed.

When driving in the mountains, it is essential to stay in your lane. Don't swing wide or cut across the center of the road. Drive slow enough to let you stay in your own lane. As you go over the top of a hill be alert. There could be an accident or some obstruction in your lane.

Be aware of all highway signing which warn of special problems. Examples are long grades, passing and no-passing zones, falling rocks, or winding roads. Be alert and take appropriate action.

For the most part, the *superslabs*, (Interstate highways), have grades which do not exceed 6 to 7 percent. Translated, this means you go up, or down, 6 feet in elevation for every 100 feet forward. This doesn't sound like much, but a 30,000 pound coach starting down a 6% grade at 50 miles per hour can reach a speed of 75 mph in about two miles if no compression brakes are engaged or the engine is not downshifted.

The following anecdotes are some of our experiences with mountain driving.

We hadn't had our first bus long. In fact,

it was just barely livable with the interior almost finished. The outside looked terrible. Part of the paint had been stripped and some of it had been sanded and other parts of the outside was spotted with body repair filler. Since it was being readied for painting, the outside looked like a disaster.

Being totally prideless I insisted that we attend a Bus Bash in Fresno, California, sponsored by the National Bus Trader Magazine. I believe this was in 1981. We did, and were parked kind of around the corner next to the side of a building almost out of sight. Although our coach looked horrible, I was very proud of what we had. Somewhere between forty and sixty converted buses attended. I was absolutely dazzled at the beauty and luxury of most of these buses. It certainly gave me a target to work toward.

After that weekend was over, in consultation with my copilot, Roberta, we decided since we were so close, we would explore Sequoia National Park. This was a straight shot due east of Fresno, less than forty miles, so it was a natural thing to do.

Now it should be said that this old bus of ours had it's original four speed manual transmission and was devoid of power steering. In fact looking back on it, I believe that it was equipped with anti-power steering. Or so it seemed.

We began our ascent into these mountains and the process was a little more than I had bargained for. We were, however, committed. So onward we went and I was getting more and more nervous. Finally we arrived at Lodgepole, a small village at the center of the park where we stopped and had lunch.

After lunch we got back in the bus and I tried starting it. Nothing! It wouldn't start. Oh my gosh, what will I do? I got out and ran around to the back and looked at the engine. I didn't know what to look for. I went back to the front and tried to start it again. It started! Whatever I did in the back, which was nothing, worked! I had to remember this. I later dubbed this, *The Motor Stare Repair.*

Before continuing our journey, I spoke with a park ranger. I explained that I was new to being a bus driver and asked him if there was a simpler way to return to civilization. He assured me that if I were to continue down the mountain toward Visalia I would find it shorter, and less nerve-rack-ing, than the way we had come.

With this assurance, we confidently proceeded toward Visalia. We began our descent trusting that shortly we would reach Visalia and begin our way home southward on highway 99. The road was quite benign in the beginning but it quickly developed into a rather steep descent. Suddenly the curves became sharper than we had previously seen.

I remember many right-hand curves that were so sharp we were forced to go into the oncoming lane to negotiate them. Several times I could feel the side of the bus brush by a tree on the right. Then we came to a series of hairpin turns and the ones to the right had to be twice as tight as the left-hand turns. More than once I was forced to stop and back up so that I might make a turn to the right. In several instances this occurred while oncoming traffic was waiting for us to get out of the way. This will live in my memory forever as one of the most nerve shattering experiences of my life

Finally we reached a straightaway. It looked as if we were getting out of the mountains at last. We came around a bend and there in front of us was one of those drive-through trees in the middle of the road. Only the hole through the tree was the size of a Volkswagen and we were a bus bigger than an ocean liner! Oh my Gawd! I can't turn around let alone go back up the way we came! As we reached this holed tree, mercifully we spotted a dirt road going around it and this we took. A little later we reached Visalia and pulled into a shopping center and parked near one end. I knocked some of the bark off the right side fenders and shakily got out some camp chairs and a twelve-pack of beer. About forty-five minutes later our nerves, which were on end, finally started to curl over and relax a little.

One time we were returning from the East by way of Route I-40. Instead of going through Needles, California we decided to head south from Flagstaff, Arizona toward I-10. Since our home was in Riverside, this appeared to be a little closer. I-10 goes through our sister city of San Bernardino.

The logical way to get to I-10 from Flagstaff is due south to Phoenix then turn right. Examining the map convinced me that we should go through Prescott and onto highway 60 so we would intersect I-10 on a diagonal. This was more or less the hypotenuse of the triangle; obviously shorter than the two sides. This was not a good idea.

We left Flagstaff, went through Sedona and on through Cottonwood. This was a rather pleasant and scenic route. As we left Cottonwood in a westerly direction, we were more than half way to Prescott. A few miles later we came to Jerome.

We made a ninety degree turn due south as we approached Jerome. As we made this turn, we saw a sign with the symbol of a truck, a red circle and a red slash through it. Now everybody knows that the red circle and red slash means it's a no-no. I made a comment to my copilot that it sure is lucky that we are not a truck. If we were, we might have to turn around.

We continued south for about a mile or so. As we did, we began to climb a rather steep grade. It was obvious that in front of us was a rather high mountain. But anyone who has approached the Virgin River Gorge from the Arizona side knows that as you approach a seemingly impenetrable wall of a mountain, magically it opens up with a negotiable passage. We were confident this would happen to what was in front of us.

As we continued to climb, the road

became steeper and steeper. We noticed off to our right a switchback, some hundred feet above us. "Oh! My Gosh! In a minute or so, we will be up there!" I said to Roberta. These switchbacks continued for several miles as we climbed from the desert floor to more than 4,000 feet.

Finally, we entered the town of Jerome. This is a town built on a cliff-side. From one street level to the next was a difference in elevation of about 50 feet or so. Every house and structure in the town had a panoramic view of Flagstaff and/or the Grand Canyon, despite the fact they were 50 to 100 miles away. Parking was nonexistent. Especially for a big rig like a converted bus. I then realized that the little no-no sign at the bottom of the ascent to Jerome also meant vehicles like ours.

At last we crept our way out of town without causing any major damage to either us or the town. We were about to heave a sigh of relief (note: all sighs of relief are heaved), when we were stopped by a highway flagger (one of those guys or gals with red flags that make you stop). Being seated just a little above most drivers we could see that the Arizona Highway Department (they may be called Az-Trans, like Cal-Trans in California) had decided it was time to re-pave this road.

It should also be pointed out that this highway was of strategic importance to the State of Arizona. Otherwise, the people of Cottonwood and Sedona would have to travel 20 miles further saving an hour while traveling to Prescott. So for about 20 or 30 minutes we admired the paving equipment owned by Arizona. Then this cute looking flagger (of course, she was a girl!) , let us continue.

It was at this point my nerves (which had calmed down from the ascent to Jerome) started standing on end. The lane that was being paved was the inside lane next to the mountain. We were directed to the outside lane. Did I mention that these lanes were only about six feet wide? Obviously this is not true since the bus has a tread width of nearly eight feet, so I will amend this statement to read, *eight feet wide?* As I drove along this outside lane away from the mountain, I could see the Gulf of California and parts of the Panama Canal. This was, of course when I could take my eyes away from the road which dropped off at a ninety degree angle straight down!

Happily this narrow, drop-off, outside lane only lasted for several hundred miles (translated three miles). As we went by the road paving machine, which was green, we left a small blue streak on it, which was the color of our bus. The road to Prescott was a delightful change with only five hundred switch-backs and down hill all the way.

Looking back on this experience, we wouldn't ever drive our bus through Jerome again for a thousand dollars. And, we would not take a hundred thousand dollars for the memory.

Another road sticks in my memory. This one is in Mexico. On the trip down Baja California about half way to Cabo San Lucas you come to Santa Rosalia. Santa Rosalia is a fishing and cannery town; a fascinating place to visit. About ten miles north of San Rosalia, just as you are approaching the Gulf of California, a downgrade of about three miles takes you to the beach. Now when I say downgrade, I mean **DOWNGRADE!**

This road which is a two lane highway, one lane each direction, twists and turns and goes down at the rate of somewhere in the neighborhood of twelve to fifteen percent. Does this sound steep to you? Think of some of the steepest grades in the U.S. and we have the Eisenhower Tunnel in Colorado, Cajon Pass and the Grapevine in California, Snowquamish in Washington, and Jerome in Arizona. These grades just mentioned seldom exceed eight percent at their steepest. If you ever decide to travel down the Baja, be prepared for this grade. Shift into your low gear and take it easy.

Driving in Weather

As to driving in snow or on ice, don't! Where your tires meet the road, most of the time you will have good traction. However, when there is snow or ice between your tires and the road, you can have a very slippery situation. You will have a lot less grip and will need to be very careful.

The worst condition is *wet ice*. Very cold snow or ice can be slick and hard to drive on, but *wet ice* can be more trouble-some because it offers the least traction of all. Wet ice occurs when it is freezing (32°F, or 0°C.)and freezing rain begins to fall. Allow much greater following distances to other vehicles. Watch for slippery spots.

If you are caught in a blizzard, pull over and stop. Try to get off the road. If you cannot get off the road, turn on your hazard flashers and tie a red cloth to your rig to alert the police you have been stopped by the snow. Keep the coach warm and if necessary run your generator to maintain power. Check your generator air intake and exhaust periodically to make sure it is not blocked by the snow. Turn on your radio for weather information and try to relax.

Blizzards often don't last much more than a day or so and if you are on a well traveled highway, a snow plow will be along when it can.

If you get stuck in the mud or soft sand do not spin your wheels. They will just dig a deeper hole.. Do not allow your wheels to spin faster than 35 mph or your tires could explode. If you have chains, use them and remove them as soon as practical. I have seen many coaches with the wheel wells and sides damaged severely due to whipping chains. Try to achieve traction with rocks, brush or other debris. One of the most effective techniques for getting un-stuck is to let the air out of your tires. Even if you have to drive 20 or thirty miles on low tires, it is often better than paying $150 to $300 for a tow truck. Also, many times a tow truck will be unable to do the job and you have to find someone with a D8 Caterpillar tractor. The story which follows is an event which occurred in Mexico.

A few years ago we were traveling in Mexico in a caravan with a couple of other coaches and when we got to Mazatlan we discovered that our favorite trailer park was full. So where were we going to park for the night? We only needed one night since we planned to travel on to Puerto Vallarta.

Bill in the *Eagles Quest* suggested that we go to the *free beach* to spend the night. That sounded like a great idea so off we went. Now for those of you who don't know where the *free beach* is, I am almost reluctant to reveal this closely guarded secret. It lies at the extreme north end of the hotel and condo row fronting the Pacific Ocean.

The *free beach,* as of this writing, is probably no longer free since as word gets around some enterprising Mexican national is no doubt capitalizing on this location, building a luxurious, high-rise expensive hotel.

Bill and Phil proceeded us onto the *free beach* with their coaches, got located and I soon followed. Not being totally satisfied with the spot left to me, I decide to relocate for just a little better view of the harbor. As I was maneuvering I went over a small sand dune and , “Uh Oh! I didn’t seem to be moving any more.”

Getting out of the coach and going back to the rear of the bus I noticed that my driver wheels on the right side seemed to be sunk a little into the sand. About this time a group of other RV dwellers on the *free beach* came over to see the commotion and to offer their help and advice. One of them said, “I’ve got a shovel,” and ran off to get it. Another said, “I’ll get some driftwood and scraps to jam under the wheels.”

I appreciated all this attention and help and was appropriately embarrassed and filled with contrition. The shovel arrived, so I started digging and stuffing (debris that it). So I would shovel, and stuff, and cuss, then try to move the bus. Nothing! Back to shoveling and stuffing and cussing, and trying to move the bus. This went on for about fifteen or twenty minutes. IT WOULDN'T MOVE!!! The driver wheels just casually spun in this hole and occasionally would spit out some of the debris that I had carefully placed.

The Irish blood coursing through my veins was getting hotter and hotter! I was putting on a more interesting performance than these casual onlookers expected. Quite a crowd was gathering. Bill and Phil were considering selling tickets. Phil started passing the hat.

Finally, in total frustration I sat down and stared at the offending hole dug by the driver wheels and myself and decided that the hole needs to be filled up rather than dug out by all this shoveling and stuffing. What would be the alternative? I thought about trying to jack up the bus but there wasn't a firm base for the jack. Soft sand was everywhere. What could I do?

Then I noticed the bogie wheel, the one just in front of the driver wheels that reside in this now infamous hole. It seems to be resting on a slight mound so I started to dig under it in an effort to lower it thus adding more weight to the drivers. This went on for another ten minutes, to no avail.

Bill suggested that I let the air out of the bogie tire, so in total frustration, I did just that. As I deflated the tire, I watched as the bus settled lower and lower and wondered if I would ever get out of this mess with less than a D-8 Caterpillar and a half-inch chain. So, back into the bus I go and start it up. Carefully I put it in gear and magically and effortlessly the bus drives away from this mean and nasty old hole.

A resounding cheer went up from the bleachers and you would have thought that I had just scored a touchdown at the Superbowl. The whole performance was certainly worth more than the price of admission to the *free beach* as many of these denizens spent months in semi-boredom at this location away from the higgley piggley furor of life up in the States.

As an epilog to this story, it was a simple matter to add air pressure to the deflated tire since I carried an air hose I could connect to my air system in case I wanted to blow up an air mattress, or some such.

Road Rage

A new phenomenon is arising as we approach the new millennium: *road rage.* People have been flipping each other the “bird”, off and on, since I was a kid, but in recent years weapons have come on the scene. I was absolutely astonished once when a guy in a Porche convertible swerved in front of my 36,000 pound rig and flipped me off. “Like, wha’d I do. . .?” All I was doing was minding my own business, staying in my own lane and moving with the traffic.

Too many impatient four-wheelers

have no concept of the potential problems which might arise from tangling with a big rig, whether it is a motor coach or a semi-truck. It is true we are equipped with larger brakes and air-cans for actuation, but a big rig will still take nearly ten times the distance to stop that a four-wheeler will. People who drive small cars (and all cars are small compared to our coaches), need to be aware of 30,000 lbs x 66 ft/sec is equal to a momentum nearly two million foot-pounds per second. To be hit by that much energy, can really ruin your day.

A good rule to follow is to exercise patience, patience and patience. For the most part, we should always be cruising in the outside lane (shoulder side) of a multiple lane highway. One of the problems with occupying the outside lane is it is the merging lane for on ramps. When going through Dallas or Los Angeles, the second inboard lane will be the easiest lane to travel. There will be no stopping for merging traffic and it is not the *ticket lane*. The *ticket lane* on a three lane highway is the inside lane; on a four lane highway it is the two inside lanes. In California, never travel the *ticket lane* while towing a car, or you'll get a ticket.

If some guy gets kind of pushy, and you can see he is getting aggravated, back off; let him have his way. He might have a Magnum in his glove compartment and there is nothing worse than being Dead Right. That too, will mess up your day.

This next message is mildly off the subject but is a somewhat appropriate history lesson.

Before the Battle of Agincourt in 1415, the French, anticipating victory over the English, proposed to cut off the middle finger of all captured English soldiers. Without the middle finger it would be impossible to draw the renowned English longbow and, therefore, be incapable of fighting in the future. This famous weapon was made of the native English Yew tree, and the act of drawing the longbow was known as "plucking the yew" (or "pluck yew").

Much to the bewilderment of the French, the English won a major upset and began mocking the French by waving their middle fingers at the defeated French, saying, "See, we can still pluck yew! PLUCK YEW!"

Over the years some 'folk etymologies'

have grown up around this symbolic gesture. Since ‘pluck yew’ is rather difficult to say (like “peasant mother pheasant plucker,” which is who you had to go to for the feathers used on the arrows for the longbow), the difficult consonant cluster at the beginning has gradually changed to a labiodental fricative ‘F’ and thus the words often used in conjunction with the one-finger-salute are mistakenly thought to have something to do with an intimate encounter.

It is also because of the pheasant feathers on the arrows that the symbolic gesture is known as “giving the bird.”

And yew all thought yew knew everything!

Towing

Towing a car behind our motor coach increases your pleasure, versatility and safety, immensely. This is virtually equivalent to having a yacht with it's tender so you may park your coach and go ashore or to the movies or shopping or sight seeing or to an emergency room if necessary.

A number of rules go along with towing. In most states you are restricted to obeying the traffic laws set up for large semi-trucks. For example most states require a towing vehicle to maintain 55 mph or less.

Further rules are, you must stay in the outside lane except when passing and on a highway with more than two lanes, you may not use more than the two outside lanes. This is not a hard and fast rule for all states. It is for California. My approach is if it works for California it should work everywhere. This is not true in all states, however. Pennsylvania and West Virginia still enforce the national 55 mph statute repealed by most states. It is a good idea to check in with a state welcome, or information rest stop and learn the idiosyncracies of that state. After all, traffic enforcement is a great source of local revenue and who doesn't need revenue?

When towing, you must wire your towed vehicle to respond to all the normal signals of the towing vehicle. When you step on the brake, your towed car must illuminate its stop lights. When your turn signals are switched on, so must your car show the right or left blinker light. When your marker lights go on, your cars tail lights must also light.

This project is fairly easy with a 12 volt DC electrical system on your coach. When your coach is set up with a 24 volt

DC system, a series of relays must be inserted in the system to actuate the towed car lights. A typical wiring diagram is shown for both the 12 VDC and 24VDC electrical systems in the chapter on circuits.

Today's tow bars are a real advancement from the old rigid tow bar where your mate had to carefully inch the car up to the coach, then squirm the car back and forth until the socket hitch was lined up over the ball hitch. No brand names will be mentioned but several tow bars are now manufactured to allow you to get within a square foot window to hook up to the coach. This means all you have to do, is get reasonably close, which you may gauge from your car seat. Then get out of your car and drop the hitch onto the ball and secure it. After engaging your safety chains and plugging in your electrical umbilical, all you have to do is drive away in the coach and the hitch frame extends and locks into place.

Another new towing device is permanently mounted to the coach frame and you drive your car close and then an adjustable window is available to engage the car and the same conditions apply as above. The principle advantage to this system is that there is no unsightly mechanism hanging on your tow car.

The umbilical cord is the electrical connection between the coach and the car. A rather neat umbilical cord is the one which is coiled like a telephone so that it expands and contracts into a sanitary package. The safety chain, or cable must be at least ¼ chain or 3/16 wire rope. I personally use 3/16 inch wire rope with a plastic coating. The plastic coat makes it easy to clean and your chain or cable will get dirty while it does it's job.

The first time I heard of tow-car problems, was when a friend of mine, who took his bus to Portland to be converted, was returning to Southern California. At one point along I-5, he pulled off the interstate to have lunch. While he was enjoying his sandwich an Oregon State Trooper came up to him and asked if he had lost a Volkswagen. Puzzled, Carl went outside to look at his newly completed conversion to discover his tow-car was not attached. The trooper then informed him that they had found a VW off the road in a ditch with a tow bar attached and he had been inquiring at each off ramp since to find the owner. So Carl got in the patrol car and rode back to the scene and there was his tow-car. It had no damage as the hitch had simply come loose from the bus. The car had careened into the ditch with a lot of tall grass which had cushioned its stop. He simply backed it out of the ditch, drove it back, hooked up and finished his sandwich.

Another incident comes to mind. Bob and Phyllis, after converting an old GMC SILVERSIDES, had gone all the way to Panama just to prove they could do it. As a tow-car, they had a Volkswagen *Thing*, a sort of rugged boxy convertible jeep-like vehicle. As the trip progressed, Bob seemed to develop a bit of animosity toward the *Thing*. On their way back to the States, they were in Guatemala, fording a small river (water level up to the axles), with the *Thing* securely (they thought) fastened to the rear of their coach. On reaching the other side of the stream, several Indians were being very demonstrative, trying to get their attention, so Bob finally pulled over. He got out and went back to discover, no *Thing*. After much gesturing and pidgin communication, they hired a boat and went down stream to discover the *Thing* hung up on a sand bar. It had floated almost a half mile until it was snagged by this sand bar. So, Bob got in and with the help of some rope and some Indians got the vehicle across the river. It started, so he was able to drive it to the coach, reconnect it, and continue their trip home with the *Thing*.

The two examples above are illustrations of the result of failing to be sure that safety chains or cables are adequately secured. Something that happened to us one time was a little different. We had a tow car that used a rigid yoke shaped tow bar. The tow bar was removable, so rather than drive around with the tow bar attached and perched up in the air, I would remove it each time I disconnected from the bus. It was reattached to the car with clevis pins secured with those hairpins style cotter pins made from spring steel

Once, while getting ready to return home from Oregon, I noticed that I had lost one of the hairpin style cotter pins. No problem, I simply grabbed some bailing wire, stuck it through the cotter pin hole in the clevis pin, gave it a twist figuring that'll do the job, so off we went.

As we were traveling through the California Redwoods between Crescent City and

Eureka, I kept noticing a car in my mirror that looked a little like our tow-car, trying to pass us on the curves. A very dangerous maneuver, indeed. Finally, on one really tight turn, I got a really good look at that car that kept pestering me, and OH MY GOSH! It was our tow-car!

Now, the highway deep in the Redwoods ranges from narrow to very narrow, with almost no turnouts. We finally came to a very narrow turnout, so I pulled over. Even before I got out of the coach, I heard several truckers on the CB radio complaining about that stupid motorhome driver picking such a dumb place to park. I walked back to discover that the clevis pin I had secured with that twist of bailing wire, was gone, and the tow bar was connected to the car at only one side and had bent ninety degrees so that the car was sticking out on the driver's side. With some degree of difficulty, I managed to disconnect the car from the bus, then removed the tow bar from the car. We were not in the most convenient location, so Roberta then drove the car to the nearest town where I followed and had a chance to spend some time to straighten out the bent clevis. Later, of course, a more permanent remedy was achieved.

About two years ago, we were enjoying the Albuquerque Balloon Festival with a gang of friends in a coach caravan, and about four or five coaches decided to run up to Santa Fe to see the sights. On the way back we all decided to refuel in Albuquerque, then continue on our way to Phoenix for a bus rally. Jack in the Spam Can, a converted GMC Superior, mentioned over the CB that he may be getting a little low on fuel but he thought he could probably make it to the truck stop in Albuquerque. We were all at a fuel pump, or waiting for an open bay, when Jack pulled into the truck stop. Lucky for him, there was an open bay, so he headed for the pump. About that time his coach stopped, out of fuel. Being a canny guy, Jack sent his beloved, Jean, back to the tow-car, a VW van. Jean got in the van, started it and pushed the bus to the fuel pump as Jack steered, thereby converting the tow-car into a push-car.

One other Jack and Jean event occurred when they were about two blocks from home, were about to pass under the freeway but waiting for a stop light. As the light changed, they proceeded on their way when all kinds of commotion broke out. People began blowing their horns, shouting at them and gesturing. So they slowed down to find out what was happening. It seems that as they left the stop light in their bus, their tow-car stayed parked. Some tow-car fun!

Finally, I am reminded of the time I drove into a rally at the Phoenix Dog Races parking lot. We got out and were greeted by all our friends. We then spent a few minutes saying hello and getting brought up to date on the latest news. And, we had to relate our experiences about our trip over from Albuquerque which was rather uneventful.

I then went around to the back of the coach to disconnect the car. This was usually a simple matter and as I was folding up the tow bar, Carl reached down to my tow hitch on the bus, picked up the ball and handed it to me. Somewhere over the last two or three hundred miles the nut securing the hitch ball had fallen off, and incredibly, the ball remained in place with just the stud through the hole. We had towed our car an indeterminable number of miles on a ball that was nutless.

This is certainly a testimonial for the smooth ride of the Eagle coach, or to the highways of the western United States. God must forgive a lot of stupidity!

See Appendix Page 385 for state Towing Laws

With reference to the state towing charts in the appendix on page 383, 384 and 385, some comments should be made.

Virtually all states require the following items to be in place on towed vehicles:

1. Safety chains
2. Stops Lights
3. Tail Lights
4. Clearance Lights
5. License Plate Lights
6. Turn Signals

The only three items mandatory during daylight towing are safety chains, stop lights and turn signals. Trailer brakes do not apply when towing a car, however many states require breakaway brakes.

Some states permit two trailers to be towed. Why would this apply to motor coaching? This would be the case if you wanted to tow a car and a boat behind the car. 24 of the 50 states permit two trailers but I consider it a somewhat sporty and dangerous practice for the weekend motor coacher.

Almost every state requires insurance on the towed vehicle, but as responsible and affluent readers, we would have liability insurance anyway.

Camping

Camping needs no explanation. In recent years ,however, a term known as *dry camping* has come into use. Some might think this means to camp in the desert. Or it may mean to camp when it's not raining. Actually, it refers to camping without the advantage of electricity, water hookups and sewer dumps. In other words, it is simply old fashioned camping!

In this modern age of RV Parks, so many facilities are available, the term camping is a misnomer. In today's parks, not only are water, electricity and sewer offered, but we can also expect cable television, telephone service, recreational rooms, swimming pools and a convenience store. Can this be called camping? I would call it resort parking.

Several things should be considered when planning a camping trip. If you are planning to really camp, this means you will not have the advantage of a convenience store so all the things you might need on a trek up Mount Everest should be taken along. Almost any modern motor coach has the capacity to carry enough food and water to last a couple of weeks for a family. Unless you park next to a stream or lake, a few of the family members might reek a little. Probably the main thing to remember, is to arrive with full water tanks and empty holding tanks.

It is becoming harder and harder to find that pristine wilderness beside a bubbling stream with jumping trout you can nab for breakfast. Almost any place where you can camp in that sort of environment, is now a government park. That is, a city, regional, state, national or provincial park. Some of these parks, are fabulous camping sites.

Many of them have no facilities except a place to park your coach. Some will have electricity.

These government sponsored parks are too numerous to list. However, the National Parks offer a Golden Age Passport to seniors so they may camp for half price.

Golden Passports

Pursuant to the Land and Water Conservation Fund Act (Title 16 United States Code 460 l et seq.), visitors who use federal facilities and services for outdoor recreation, may be required to pay a greater share of the cost of providing those opportunities than the population as a whole. Under the guidelines and criteria established by law and regulation, the National Park Service will collect recreation fees of the appropriate type for its parks, facilities, and programs. No fees will be collected under circumstances where the costs of collection would exceed revenue or where prohibited by law or regulation. Fees will be reasonable and will be determined in accordance with the criteria and procedures contained in the Land and Water Conservation Fund Act and Regulations in Title 36 Code of Federal Regulations.

The government has established the

Golden Eagle, Golden Age and Golden Access Passports that, when obtained, allow the public to enter fee areas without additional charge. This is very convenient when traveling to several areas that charge an entrance fee. Please note that the passports are nontransferable. They can not be loaned to someone else. The pass belongs to the person who signs it.

Golden Eagle Passport

This is an entrance pass to those national parks, monuments, historic sites, recreation areas, and national wildlife refuges that charge an entrance fee. The Golden Eagle Passport costs $50 and is valid for one year from date of purchase. You may purchase a Golden Eagle Passport at any NPS entrance fee area or by mail. To purchase by mail send a $50 check or money order (do not send cash) to: **National Park Service,** 1100 Ohio Drive, SW Room 138, Washington, DC 20242 Attention: Golden Eagle Passport

The Golden Eagle Passport admits the pass-holder and any accompanying passengers in a private vehicle. Where entry is not by private vehicle, the passport admits the pass holder, spouse, children, and parents. The Golden Eagle Passport does not cover or reduce use fees, such as fees for camping, swimming, parking, boat launching, or cave tours. It is valid for entrance fees only.

Golden Age Passport

This is a lifetime entrance pass for those 62 years or older. The Golden Age Passport has a one time processing charge of $10. You must purchase a Golden Age Passport in person (it is not available by mail or telephone). This can be done, at any NPS entrance fee area. At time of purchase you must show proof of age (be 62 years or older) and be a citizen or permanent resident of the United States. The Golden Age Passport admits the pass-holder and any accompanying passengers in a private vehicle. Where entry is not by private vehicle, the passport admits the pass holder, spouse, children, and parents. The Golden Age Passport also provides a 50% discount on federal use fees charged for facilities and services such as fees for camping, swimming, parking, boat launching, or cave tours. It does not cover or reduce special recreation permit fees or fees charged by concessionaires

Golden Access Passport

This is a free lifetime entrance pass for persons who are blind or permanently disabled. It is available to citizens or permanent residents of the United States, regardless of age, who have been determined to be blind or permanently disabled. You may obtain a Golden Access Passport at any entrance fee area by showing proof of medically determined disability and eligibility for receiving benefits under federal law. The Golden Access Passport admits the passholder and any accompanying passengers in a private vehicle. Where entry is not by private vehicle, the passport admits the pass holder, spouse, children, and parents. The Golden Access Passport also provides a 50% discount on federal use fees charged for facilities and services such as fees for camping, swimming, parking, boat launching, or cave tours. It does not cover or reduce special recreation permit fees or fees charged by concessionaires.

Making Camp

The idea of making camp is to get everything set up so all you have to do is lay back and fish. This also means your camping mate can also lay back and fish. This does not mean once you squirmed your way into your parking place you are done. No sir, get the coach as level as you can, get out the camping chairs, lay out the camping carpet, extend the awning and, if you have power available, hook up.

The normal sequence of events is ;

1. Move your coach into it's assigned spot. Back and fill several times to miss that tree. Be sure and leave lots of room for your picnic table. Be careful you don't block one of your cargo doors. Try to squirm over a smidge so you have a better view of the water.

2. Level your coach. If you have hydraulic levels this is a snap. Otherwise get out your blocks and guess how many are needed under each wheel. Have your camping mate outside to warn you when you are about to drive off your blocks. Once you are up on your blocks, check your level and start over. You could also use a couple of bottle jacks instead of leveling blocks and this way you position them and pump them up. Then you go inside and put your test level on the floor crosswise and lengthwise. If it looks OK, you're done, otherwise, start

ing pumping again.

3. Next you have to extend the entry step or get out the milk crate you carry to boost you up to the door.

4. Pull the camping carpets out of the cargo hold and unroll them. After positioning them, be sure to find some decent size rocks to lay on each corner so the wind doesn't blow them away.

5. Go around and pull down all your window awnings and secure them in place. Now go to work on that cantankerous patio awning. Snag it and pull it down. Then go to work at each end, pushing it out one notch at a time. Then do the same at the other end. Do this back and forth until it is all the way out. Finally plant the uprights on the ground and find some bigger rocks to keep them in place. They always give you those foot long nails to secure your uprights but I have never found any ground that you could drive them into.

6. Get out your camping chairs and your little bitty chip and dip tables to set along side.

7. Go around to the other side of the coach and pull out your umbilical cord (another name for your shore power cord). If

this is a 50 amp cord it is about as easy to handle as a fire hose under pressure. Find the adapter you need (you will have approximately 23 combinations of various amp ratings to fit other amp ratings). This might take a little while so you may want to take a break and have a beer. Finally, you are plugged in.

8. Unwind your garden hose and connect it to the pedestal. Some places are sneaky and a common garden variety connection will not work. Then you have to go to the registration office and put down a deposit for a special fitting you will forget to return. This is obviously a sneaky conspiracy to peddle defective connectors which will not work anywhere else.

9. At this point, a lot of people hook up their sewer hose (we always call it a dump hose, like there is something dirty about a *sewer* hose). I prefer to wait until we are about to leave, then I hook up my dump hose and let 'er all fly at once. I have the feeling this process is beneficial to the holding tank, unknown , of course, to the tank.

10. Finally, we should crank up our antenna or position our satellite dish to re-

mind us we are not really camping.

11. The last thing on this menu is to mix a drink, or grab a beer, and get out the chips and dip. We are now ready to get acquainted with our neighbors and begin the process of exchanging lies.

De-Camping for Dummies

Breaking camp has to be easy, doesn't it? Well, there are a few things you should keep in mind and try to avoid. And, I can speak from experience since I have done 'em all. It is sometimes known as "brain-lockup." Anyhow, here is a list with some lessons.

1. Always try to remember to unplug your electrical shore line.

2. Always try to remember to retract your TV antenna. Once I put a little Garfield Doll on the steering wheel as a reminder. It got in my way so I took it off and forgot the

antenna.

3. It is a real good idea to disconnect your dump hose before driving off, especially if your dump valve is open.

4. You should almost never leave a camp site with your water hose still connected.

5. Don't drive with your awnings out. It causes to much aerodynamic resistance.

The little story which follows will graphically illustrate the main problems associated with some of the points listed above.

Ups and Downs

The title shown above is pertinent to two items on every converted bus, motorhome, camper, trailer, or any other form of RV. These two items are the television antenna and the electrical umbilical cord. Now, to tell little stories about leaving my TV antenna up while leaving an area, would be so mundane and boring, they are not worth repeating. After all, if you have done much traveling in an RV, you could probably rival my stories with a few of your own. Check with RV supply stores and you will learn that one of their most popular items is a replacement quadrant for the elevation mechanism of the most popular TV antenna. So, I simply refuse to bore the reader with a number of TV antenna destruction derbies.

The electrical umbilical cord is another common disaster among RVers. And, it is not something that happens only once. It too must be repeated many times. Probably, the most common occurrence is when you have been staying at a park, or even at home. You simply drive off with the cord still plugged into the outlet. Often somebody will yell at you and you will stop and correct the situation. Sometimes the plug is a little deformed, but a little work with a pair of pliers will straighten it out. Other times the cord will drag on the pavement for miles and lo and behold, no plug.

Having experienced this event more times than I wish to admit, I have become very conscientious to roll up my umbilical and carefully stow it on it's hooks. At this point I would like to describe the way my umbilical is and its penetration through the bus. First of all, since mine is a thoroughly modern bus conversion, my umbilical is equivalent to that of a mobile home. This means it is a 50 amp cord, almost the size of a fire hose and about as flexible as a two by four stud. Second, I have a trap door in the floor of my utility compartment which will accommodate my sewer hose, umbilical cord, cable TV, water hose, and telephone line. This of course, means a careful and judicious placement of all these utilities to get them to pass through the opening. After all the various items snaking out of the floor of this compartment are returned to their place and we are ready for traveling, the trap door is closed and remains that way by gravity.

One summer we spent a few days at the Bremerton Elks Lodge in the beautiful state of Washington. We decided to head south. Tacoma, nearly fifty miles south of us, was our next destination so everything was carefully stowed. As we approached the Tacoma Narrows bridge, traffic slowed to a crawl. Apparently the road department of Washington decided it was time to do some road repair. We were on a divided road with two lanes each direction. As we sat for a while, a car came up beside us and announced that we had something dragging. Well, the traffic wasn't moving so I got out and inspected the problem. There was my umbilical with the plug end half worn away. I stuffed it back in and got back in the bus in time to move forward another twenty feet.

While settling in, after our arduous journey of about fifty miles, I went back to inspect the damage. Now a 50-amp plug has four prongs, two for each hot lead, a neutral and a ground. One of the hot lead prongs had been ground down to almost nothing. I decided that if I was careful we would be O.K. until we got home and I could replace the plug. The unexplained mystery, however, was how did that stiff umbilical manage to open that trap door against gravity and squirm it's way out of the utility compartment? Maybe Robert Stack of *Unsolved Mysteries* could attack this problem?

After returning I replaced the plug end with a replacement plug. I should have bought a whole new umbilical with the plug molded in place which would not have been much more money. In any event, after a year the common, i.e., the white wire came loose in the replacement plug and did not announce the fact. This resulted in sending 240-volts to several appliances who did not react kindly to this increased voltage. In fact, they quit working. We were unaware of this appliance revolt until we were at a rally and both the television and the microwave oven refused to operate.

I removed the TV from it's nesting place and opened it up, exposing all kinds of mysterious items. The first target was a fuse. Voila! The fuse was burned out, so I replaced it. Easy fix, huh? To prove my prowess, I plugged the TV back in and zappp, there went the new fuse. So, I used some alligator clips and jumpered around the fuse holder, then plugged it in again. Ah Ha!! Now a capacitor smoked. Off to Radio Shack I went to get a new capacitor. They did not have the one I needed, so I picked up something close. It looked about the right size and shape. After soldering the new part in I tried the TV and it worked like a charm. WOW! I'm a TV repairman!

The next project was the microwave. Since my confidence was at an all time high after successfully repairing the TV, how tough could a microwave be? Again, I had to disengage the microwave from the coach. This was a formidable job since I had to remove a cabinet in order to remove the microwave, but it was done. Now to open the electrical compartment and find the burned out fuse. Uh Oh! The fuse was still in tact. So I did a really, really clever thing. I took it to an appliance repair shop. A week later and $77 dollars lighter, I picked up the unit and reinstalled it.

Just keep one thing in mind as you travel in an RV, keep your umbilical up and your antenna down.

Full Time Motor Coaching

I am probably not qualified to discuss full time living aboard a motor coach, but many of my friends do reside in their coach full time. And, I can't help but hear their stories. A lot of Rvers are known as *Snowbirds*. This term probably began as a tag for those Canadians emulating their famous geese and heading south for the winter. The City of Yuma, Arizona, for example, just about doubles in size every winter, populated by Canadians, Oregonians, and Washingtonians. I apologize for those I left out. For a more definitive dissertation on Full Time Living Aboard, see **Living Aboard your RV, A Guide to Full Time Life on Wheels** by Janet Groene and **Cooking Aboard Your RV.** These books are available by writing to **RV Books**, Box 248, DeLeon Springs, FL 32130

Most of these full timers are ordinary citizens who vote and pay their taxes. There is, however, a segment of this group which just decided to drop out of the world of politics and taxes. Many of this group will have a mail forwarding post office or use a friend's address to get their mail. This way they can maintain insurance, a driver's license and an official identity. This way they will respond only to mail which is meaningful. They are not deluged with junk mail, offers and announcements they have won a $100,000,000 if they return the notification and buy twenty years of magazine subscriptions.

Many of this group will deal only in cash, refusing to maintain a bank account. Often an income is generated through Swap Meets and Flea Markets. Others have a talent to sell and will be a roving handyman or specialist in some trade. Cash is the preferred medium of exchange.

Other full timers will spend their days visiting friends throughout the country; spending a week or so here and another three or four weeks there. Many times we have hosted one of our full timer friends.

Most of the full timers we know will spend the summer at their children's homes, parked in the driveway or in the back yard. This way they are available for baby-sitting and can help their kids when necessary. Many of this same group will own a lot in a location in the warm country such as Yuma, South Texas, Hilton Head, or Florida. Some areas actively solicit Snowbirds by developing lots for RVs.

These lots are generally laid out for two rigs and come with electricity, sewer hookup and water. It is up to the buyer to do any paving desired. Many owners will have a small building erected between the two RV spaces. This small building will house such things as a laundry, a small workshop and a recreational area. A really neat aspect of this sort of full time RV living is being situated in a community where virtually everyone is equal, hence, much socializing takes place.

Other full timers not wishing to own

property will belong to a membership campground. There are many local private camp grounds and a few nationwide organizations. Coast-To-Coast is a membership campground which is an association of many private campgrounds. They permit parking of members for a nominal fee regardless of the member's home park. Another is Thousand Trails and NACO. These campgrounds charge no daily fee to their members. They are more like a resort park than just a campground. It is customary for full timers to stay no longer than 23 weeks at any one location. They then move to another preserve in the chain and take up residency again.

One of the items many people new to the RV life-style desire, is a washer/dryer combination. And, apartment size units are available. The main drawback to a washer/dryer in an RV is the space it occupies. Obviously, space is a premium in a motor coach. In addition, it is usable only when attached to a water and sewer hookup. It would have very little application in a camping environment such as *boondocking.*

When traveling, it is much more efficient to use a laundromat. The money spent in a laundromat is pennies compared to the cost of a built in laundry system in your coach. Not only is the space lost for this function but due to size limitations, an RV laundry system would have to be cycled many times to be equivalent to a laundromat. Of course, this is one of the reasons many of the full timers who own their own lot will have a small *Arizona Room* next to their coaches.

Rallies

Perhaps one of the major justifications for owning a motor coach is the week end rally. This is where a bunch of like minded people gather at some location for a three day, or more, party. Although there are small private groups who regularly gather for a party, the majority of rallies are sponsored by chapters of the Family Motor Coaching Association. Rallies are also sponsored by Good Sam which is a division of Trailer Life and several magazine companies. National conventions, which are nothing more than over grown rallies, are sponsored by Bus Conversion magazine, the National Bus Trader magazine and FMCA

Rallies can and have been held almost anywhere. Gatherings have been in the middle of the desert with nothing but cactus and sage brush and on deserted streets of abandoned developments. They have been in vacant lots and at the beach. Large conventions are generally held at county fairgrounds. Some smaller chapter rallies held at RV campgrounds, offer a limited number of discounted spaces. Sometimes rallies are held at the home of one of the participants. Anyplace where there is space to legally park is fair game for a rally site.

A set of rally rules have developed over the years. The first day of the rally is taken up with parking and registration. Later that afternoon, about 5 PM, an attitude adjustment hour is conducted. This is a time where the participants gather at a rally master's coach to partake of chips and dip and a little libation of their choice. The theory being, one must adjust their normal day in and day out attitude to one of a laid back, worry free mind set. That evening no dinner is planned and is the responsibility of the individual.

The next morning, coffee and pastries are often available at the coach of the trail boss, another name for the rally master. Later in the morning a meeting might be held to discuss future rallies, thank every one for this rally, or just pass the time. Other activities may be planned during the day, such as a swap meet or a white elephant exchange. That evening, it is customary for everyone to sit down to a catered dinner, pot luck, or a restaurant.

The last morning, coffee and pastries are again served and people say goodbye, slowly break camp and head home.

In the tradition of the old West, a wagon circle is normally formed with the rally master's coach, (host, or trail boss) being the keystone to the circle. The assistant trail bosses' coaches are then parked perpendicular to the host's coach and a final coach is parked to close the square. The rest of the coaches are then lined up on this square. At this point, I must clarify that a four sided circle is a square, hence the wagons are circled.

At a large national convention, as many as 6,000 or more motor coaches have been parked. In this case, each coach is allotted approximately a 16 by 40 space on a diagonal forming a chevron configuration. I have seen large regional rallies when the coaches are parked nose to tail in a line with enough space between so a rig may pull out and leave if necessary. At any large gathering with coaches parked so close, there is always the hazard of fire and the rigs being hemmed in so they cannot escape.

We have gone on trips in our coach which have been over two and a half months to as short as a few days. After 8 to 10 weeks, the bus seems like home and the list of have-to-do items grows a little each day. Have-to-do-items are those little things that have to be attended to after you get home and you have all your tools and your fabulous workshop facilities. They are not quite in the same category as Round Tuits. Round Tuits are those little repairs and upgrades on your list that you'll do when you get a Round Tuit. Have-to-do-items are mandatory, like replacing a broken windshield, or fixing a water heater that's not working, or plugging a leak in your black water tank. Round Tuits are adding luxury items such as carpeting, or a water heater.

But, I digress. When packing for a two to three month trip, the natural inclination is to imagine your are embarking on a long sea voyage with no chance of ever seeing a corner drug store again, let alone a supermarket. You make every effort to include everything you might possibly need in an emergency. Your booze locker is totally stocked as though you are entering a strange country with prohibition still in force. You pack all the clothes you might need in all climates, despite the fact that parkas are rarely seen in Mexico, or tank tops and go-aheads are useful in the Yukon. After weeks of planning and scheming and placement, you are finally packed and ready to meet any challenge the road could present.

Now, let's examine the weekend rally. This is a little event that rarely exceeds 200 miles from home. In fact, the last one I attended was a total of 2 miles from home. These weekend rallies are the heart and soul of the busing movement. These are the events which foster camaraderie and an exchange of new and novel ideas. These are the events that train bus wives to recognize their husband's butts. These are the events that promote new and novel solutions to old and trite problems. So, how do you pack for a weekend rally?

After eaves dropping on a number of bus wives, there is no doubt in my mind it requires just as much effort to pack for a weekend rally as it does if you are leaving on a 20,000 mile circuit of the North American continent, avoiding all supermarkets and drug stores. In fact, it is a feminine bus axiom: ***It takes just as much effort to pack for a weekend as it does for a six-week trip.*** I challenge any red-blooded American, married (or, not) motor coach driver to swear he has never heard this axiom! Twenty years of planning trips in motorhomes and in a bus have demonstrated the necessity of leaving a rally, arriving home an hour or two later, and immediately unpacking only to begin packing for the next rally scheduled in six weeks. Never argue with your woman!

Rally Games

Rallies, which have been mentioned before, afford all sorts of activities. In the early days they were training periods for women to recognize their men's butts. Some rallies take on quite a sophisticated flavor, such as rivaling a sea cruise. These are the rallies sponsored by the wealthy coach owners and are really near score value of a 10, especially in the eyes of the ladies. They are also quite pricey. Other rallies are designed by the trail bosses to keep everyone checking their schedule so as to be on time for the next event. These forms of rallies often have place cards at the dinner tables. Rallies of this nature require detailed planning, advanced reservation and a sizable deposit.

Then there are the laid-back rallies requiring absolutely no reservation which are often the most fun. Having served as a trail boss at this form of rally a number of times, I never stop being surprised at the attendance. In the first place, we require no reservations so we have no idea that anyone will even show up. We plan only one advertised event, such as an ice cream social. Our planning is to buy three tubs of ice cream at the warehouse discount store and the sprinkles and topping. If no one shows up, we will eventually eat it all. If too many people show up, we go get another tub or two - no big deal!

Where do we have these laid-back rallies? We often ask permission from an airport, or other sporting event such as a rodeo or car race, to park in their lot. Most of the time we are welcomed as additional customers for their events. Very often, the parking is free. We are careful to clean up the place and leave it as we found it.

Now we can't spend all our time watching skydivers, balloons and ultra light airplanes. So, how do we kill more time? Most of the time the good-old-boys sit around and hold court, that is, swapping lies about the good-old-days and impressing the newcomers. The ladies all get together and play cards. Sometimes they all go off shopping leaving all the guys to sit around impressing each other with their knowledge and wit.

One game often played is a White-Elephant swap. Although the rules are somewhat in dispute, the way it is played goes something like this. Everybody, including the kids, if there are any, wrap up an old piece of junk, or even something nice. These priceless items are placed in the center of the circle of camp chairs where everyone sits. Numbered slips of paper are given to everyone contributing a gift wrapped *white elephant.* A duplicate remains in a hat. A number is drawn from the hat and the person holding that number selects a gift. The gift is unwrapped and displayed for all to see. A new number is then drawn from the hat. The person holding that number may select an item from the center, or take a gift from a previous selector, and so on. If an item is coveted and claimed by a new selector, the third selector of that item is the ultimate possessor and it may not be taken from him/her.

Admittedly, the above described game is quite complicated, so we will list other more mundane and more sedate forms of entertainment. Bocce Ball is still popular. This is a game requiring very sophisticated equipment, such as a Bocce Ball set. Bocce, I believe, is Italian for *kiss*. The plan is to throw a small ball some distance, then see how close you can roll a larger ball to it. Each player has two colored balls and rolls them in turn. If your opponent is near the bocce, an effort is made to knock them further away from the little ball. Who ever remains the closest to the small ball wins the point. Those avid affectionados of Bocce Ball will probably cringe since they have well manicured bowling lawns on which to play. The motor coaching gang, however, will play on any surface, in any direction. I recall one time in the desert playing in and around the sage brush, in gully washes and out. When we finally looked up, we were a mile and a half from camp. It is great sport to pitch the little ball behind a tree.

Another favorite is Polish Horseshoes. In order to be more politically correct, we have eliminated the ethnic slur and now call the game, washer toss (how dull). This is a simple game using two carpeted boards with three 4-inch holes in each. Each player has a set of three 3½-inch diameter washers to toss into the holes. The toss distance is approximately ten feet. The closest hole is scored 1 and the farthest hole is scored 3. The middle hole is also scored, duh. The game can be played with only one board. It just takes a little more walking.

Pot Luck Dinners

A common form of camaraderie and social intercourse is the *pot luck*. A number of years ago, this was a favorite past time for the Bus Nuts. *Editors note: The author cleverly omitted the full name of the Bus Nuts so there will be no repercussions, lawsuits, and name calling. There are at least 8 to 12 different Bus Nut groups around the country.* At some earlier *pot luck* dinners, a few participants failed to bring their fair share of vittles. As a result, it was decreed that all members partaking of a *pot luck* affair shall bring enough to feed three times their consumption. The resulting effect was to sometimes have enough leftovers to take to the local *Guiding Light Mission.* Other times, we barely made it. It seemed some of the ladies lined their purses with baggies, and needed a dolly to return their stash to their coach.

One memorable *pot luck* was held on New Year's Day in Pasadena at the Rose Parade. Keep in mind, it becomes dark in Pasadena about five o'clock in the afternoon around that time of year. One other thing the reader should know, much to the chagrin of the Pasadena Chamber of Commerce.

It does get cold in Pasadena in the winter. In fact, the cold weather even affects Los Angeles. Now, I know you hearty souls living in Bemidji, Minnesota will scoff at our definition of cold, but when you are used to Riviera type weather most of the time, winter in Pasadena can be notable. *Editor's note to the Pasadena Chamber of Commerce: The author is just kidding! Just a feeble attempt at humor. OK?*

To continue with our narrative, we lined up with our plates and silverware about 4:45 PM. There may have been something more or less than 200 coaches at the rally. So the line stretched from Colorado Ave. to Azusa, Anaheim, or Cucamonga. I forget which. By the time we got to the serving table, it was half-past dark thirty and all the pots were cold, or empty. This was a *pot luck* that sticks in my mind, but nothing stuck to my ribs.

One other memorable *pot luck* was when an elderly widower gentleman came to a rally where a *pot luck* was planned. Feeling compelled to participate, our elderly Bus Nut stopped at a supermarket to pick something up to add to the feast.

I remember his contributions were

small triangular shaped whitish things. A number of people took them remarking they had a curiously sweetish flavor, somewhat like an apple flavor, but they had never experienced it in this form before. Most people decided they were some form of exotic gourmet food. As we learned later, they were frozen apple turnovers which our elderly gentlemen plucked out of the frozen food section, unaware they were to be cooked.

Helpful Hints By George

George Thornhill

I have been motor homing since 1965 and have driven over 600,000 miles, so most of my comments are from practical experience, either my own or some friends that I have traveled with or talked to.

SPARE PARTS

Whether you are mechanically minded or· not. I suggest that you carry a few basic spare parts. You might break down on the road or in some remote area where you can find a lot of able mechanics but no spare parts for your rig. You may be able to get parts in a day or two but if you carry some basic parts, you can save a lot of time and money. If you buy parts when you don't need them, you can shop around and save a lot compared to what you spend when you are in dire need of the parts.

I suggest that you carry spare filters, primary and secondary. You should carry a set of V belts that your engine uses and most important is a serpentine belt that a lot of new engines use. If you have your belts changed for routine maintenance, you should keep the old belts for emergency spares. If you have air suspension you should carry a spare air bag for each size your coach uses.

If your coach has air brakes, you should carry a spare diaphragm for each size your coach uses. The more spares you carry the less likely you are to need them. I having been carrying air bags and brake diaphragms for 25 years and I have never had to change any on the road but I have loaned the parts to friends who did not carry then but were broken down.

The more familiar you are with your rig the better prepared you will be to carry the important spares.

BRAKES

I believe the brakes on your coach are one of the most important systems because no matter how fast or slow you travel, you still have to stop. According to the California Vehicle Code, any vehicle over 10,000 pounds or any bus must be able to stop, from an initial speed of 20 MPH, in 40 feet. That is a short distance but any car must be able to stop in 25 feet. You don't need a calculator to see that if you are following a car going 20 MPH and you are only 15 feet away from it and that car makes a panic stop, you will hit it. When you allow for your reaction time, you may hit the car before you have a chance to apply the brakes. If you are towing a car without auxiliary braking, your stopping distance will be greatly increased because that vehicle will be pushing you. The moral of this story is **DON'T TAILGATE.**

There are two types of brakes, hydraulic and air. With hydraulic brakes the stopping distance= reaction time + braking distance but with air brakes, stopping distance = reaction time + delay time +braking distance. Air brakes take a fraction longer to operate because the air has to compress in the lines to operate the brakes.

There are several types of auxiliary braking devices for the coaches. They are Engine Compression Brake (JAKE), engine exhaust brake, drive line retarder and transmission retarder. There are advantages and disadvantages to each one. For the driver who tows a car there are several types of auxiliary braking devices for the tow vehicle. Most states require brakes on trailers over a certain gross weight. I believe that some day all states will require brakes an all towed vehicles.

FOUR WAY FLASHERS

Four way flashers are a very important part of your coach and are not for emergency use only. When you are backing up where there is a chance of people being around, use your flashers. Many coaches have backup bells or beepers but a lot of people are hard of hearing so it is good to use all the warning devices you have available. When you are entering a busy street from a parking lot or from a secondary side road, use your flashers. This is especially important when you are towing a car.

Most drivers will see you when you are entering the traffic but will not pay attention and try to pass you before you are completely on the road so they don't have to follow you. Everybody seems to be in a hurry. Flashers do not give you the right away so remember to look carefully before you make a move. Many states require slow moving vehicles to use their flashers on main thoroughfares.

TIRES

Tires are one of the most important parts of your rig. Regardless of how much horsepower your engine has or how pretty your paint job, you can't get very far on a flat tire. I know two coach owners who lost wheels from their rigs shortly after having tires changed. Most tire shops will put a notice on your receipt stating you should re-torque the wheels after 100 miles of travel. Usually it is the dual wheels that come off and I believe that it is because the inner lug nuts do not have the proper tightening torque applied before the outside wheel is installed. It is important to keep a check on tire wear and pressure. A visual check of your tires can save problems, It is hard to check on tires and wheels when you have the fancy wheel covers so you must remember to check on those tires a little closer and more thoroughly.

Many coach owners do not carry a spare tire because they believe it takes up to much room and they can't change it anyway. It is just like a spare part, you can find a lot of tire changers but tires are a little harder to find. I won't mention any names but on a trip to Baja California with several other coaches, the editor of this book had to buy a serviceable junk tire in Loreto so he could keep up with the group. (*Ed note: George was obviously thinking of another one of our group.*)

A lot of coach owners cover their tires and put a lot of different products on them to protect them. Tires will deteriorate over time and my suggestion is to wear them out before they rot. In over 600,003 miles of travel in my converted GM4104 bus, I have replaced many tires. I have seen no appreciable difference between the inside of the tire or the outside of it. Also I have seen no difference between the inside dual and the outside dual. **Why is it that when you have a flat on a dual tire it is usually the inside dual?**

(George's note: The editor has a faulty memory)

Mechanical Mysteries of Modern Motor Coaches

The modern motor coach is a mechanical marvel. It is totally self contained and as such can sustain life in remote and pristine locations for days on end. In many ways it is like a space station on earth. This earth station, with all it's wonders, can be segregated into a number of individual systems, hence rendering it simple for the average guys to understand.

Detail will be given for each system so the average owner can develop a respect for, and the ability to minimally diagnose problems as they will surely arise. According to my old buddy, *Murphy*, there is no question if a problem occurs, the question is when and where? If one had a choice, all problems with motor coaches would only occur when at home or when visiting a mechanically talented friend who loves to work on other guys' coaches..

The systems of the modern motor coach are:

1. Automotive
2. Body
3. Plumbing
4. Electrical System
    a. 120 VAC
        i. Shore Power
        ii. Generator Power
        iii. Inverter
    b. 12 VDC
5. Comfort Control
6. Equip., Appliances & Electronics
7. Gauges, Instrument and Monitors
8. Cabinet Work
9. Paint and Body
10. Furnishings

Automotive

The automotive portion of the modern motor coach ranges from that of a small car up to the complexity of a bus. Today, more and more motor coaches have diesel motors and air brakes. Additionally, more coaches are using the large tires common on the big rig trucks with ply ratings up to 16 ply.

The majority of bus engines are Detroit "71" series. This engine series began in the early "30s", and has been configured in probably more combinations than any other series engine. The designation "71" is the size of the cylinder in cubic inches. It is a two stroke engine, meaning it fires on every up stroke and exhausts on every down stroke. As a result of this action, it has almost twice the torque rating of a four cycle engine. The most common configurations for this series of engine are the in-line-six, and the V8, although industrial applications have ranges from a 2-71 to a V12-71, and many combinations in between.

In the early 70s, the "92" series became popular for bus installation, with the V6-92 replacing the V8-71, at approximately the equivalent horsepower. In addition, the newer engines became turbocharged, although many of the V8-71s have been turbo charged. The newer V6-92 has better balance and better low end torque.

Along came air pollution concerns and then standards. The two stroke engine is definitely a dirty motor so the engineers at Detroit developed computer controlled fuel systems for the 92 series. This new system was known as the D-DEC, or Detroit Diesel Electronic Computer control system. More recently, Detroit has begun marketing their new **series 60** engines for bus and truck power. This new engine is a four cycle engine and is much cleaner burning and has a very high efficiency rating.

However, many of us with older buses and limited budgets, must be content with the older engines. Fortunately, parts and kits will continue to be made for these power plants. In addition to genuine Detroit parts, there are several after market manufacturers of parts for the older engines.

The old standby engine, the V8-71, is nominally rated at 318 horsepower and delivers approximately 270 horsepower to the wheels. With this motor, pulling a long tough grade tends to tax the patience of most converted bus drivers, having to be content with 25 to 30 miles per hour. So it has become popular to upgrade to the V8-92 motor. This upgrade must also include an upgrade in cooling capacity. The bigger motor produces nearly 500 horsepower and an associated increase in heat. The simple way to increase the cooling capacity is to replace your radiator with the one recommended by the factory. In some cases, the factory no longer exists, so consult with the engine manufacturer for a recommendation. In many cases, additional radiators have been added and seem to work satisfactorily.

The standard injector size for the ***71*** series is 60, and for the ***92*** series is the 90. In many cases, additional horsepower can be achieved by increasing the size of the injectors. Furthermore, even though it seems illogical, increase in fuel economy has been achieved with the larger injectors. It is common in the Northwest for logging trucks with V6-92 engines to install 105 or 110 injectors, and get not only more power, but better fuel economy. I have discussed this with Detroit representatives who have told me, "Yes, this is true, but it will shorten your engine life." So, I make no recommendation, only reporting what I have heard.

Transmissions installed in earlier buses have always been the four speed manual shift type. Many of the earlier city transit buses used a three speed automatic, but since a city transit bus is not recommended for bus conversions, this will not be discussed (I hope nobody gets their nose out of joint, sorry).

In this country the most common automatic transmission is the Allison. The Allison transmission is virtually bulletproof. The 700 series is a heavy duty transmission and is used for semi-trucks with loads up to 80,000 pounds, and for heavy earth moving equipment. When using an V8-71 engine, the 654 Allison is a natural match. The **5** in the designated number is the number of gear ratios in the transmission. The most common automatic used against the ***92*** series engine is the Allison 740. This is a four speed heavy duty transmission. The reason a four speed transmission may be used on the ***92*** series engine is the motor has a reasonably high torque rating at low RPM. The ***71*** series engine does not achieve a usable torque until it reaches a high RPM. This means the RPM on the ***71*** must be maintained at a higher speed in order to achieve a minimum torque rating and avoid ***lugging*** the motor, hence the need for more gear splits.

The latest transmission to come on the scene is the B500 Allison World transmission. This transmission along with the new Detroit series 60 engines are now available in brand new bus shells from Eagle Coach Corporation.

For those of you on a limited budget, the ten speed manual transmission is a vast improvement over the old four speed box.

Unless you have had trucker experience, the idea of ten speeds sounds formidable but actually they are quite simple. There are five gear locations in low range, then a splitter is actuated and the same five locations are repeated. The average ten speed transmission can be picked up at a truck salvage yard for about $800 to $1,000. More recently, a nine speed unit has become popular for around the same price range. Again, the Fuller Ten Speed Road Ranger is virtually bulletproof when installed in a bus conversion. These units are made to work flawlessly in 80,000 pound semi-trucks, so a 35,000 pound bus conversion is an easy task.

One of the delightful features of the ten speed Road Ranger is the clutch is necessary to use only for starting, while idling at a stop or in moving away from a dead stop. After that, with a little practice, each gear may be shifted manually by synchronizing the move to the engine speed without the use of the clutch. In a way, it is almost like a poor-man's automatic. Another thing about the ten speed transmission is that on a flat surface, it is common to move away from a dead stop in third gear. This leaves two lower gears to use when in an awkward position, such as being parked on a hill. The old four speed box was very unforgiving when the coach was parked facing up hill. It was necessary to rev up the engine to get up enough torque, then let out the clutch to get moving. This often fried the friction material of the clutch, thus wasting it. The author bought two new clutches before he had a ten speed transmission installed in his first coach. In an up hill condition, the ten speed transmission was simply put into first gear, often called *granny gear.* The coach would then simply crawl away from a dead stop at almost walking speed.

Tires and Suspensions

Believe it or not, tires for big rigs are still available in tube type. This is hard to believe since we haven't had tube type tires on our cars for nearly thirty years. If you plan to do much travelling in Mexico, it is almost mandatory to use tube type tires with split rims. The tubeless tire is very difficult to locate, even in large cities such as Guadalajara. This was true, however, in 1991. By now, things may have changed. The tube type tires come in even designations such as, 10-20, or 11-22 and so forth.

The tube type tires can be had as radial, which have an R designation, such as 10R20. Without the R, they are bias ply tires.

The most common tires on big rigs are the radial tubeless style. They come in various load ratings, which are an extension of the load rating of automobile tires. Most big rig's tires begin with load rating "F". This is the equivalent of a 12 ply tire. The load ratings "G" and "H" are 14 and 16 ply ratings, respectively.

The most common tire on a forty foot bus is the 12.5R22.5 size. This tire fits on a 22.5 inch diameter wheel and the equivalent load rated tire on a semi-truck is the 11R24.5 tire, which fits on a 24.5 inch diameter wheel. Truck tires are almost $100 less per tire than bus tires, since so many more trucks are on the road. If you wish to continue to employ the smaller wheel, i.e., the 22.5 diameter, you may purchase the 11R22.5 truck tire in a higher load rating and still save almost $100 per tire. However, you will sacrifice a small degree of fuel economy because you are turning your motor at a specific RPM but not traveling over the ground quite as far.

If you plan to upgrade to alloy wheels

for appearance, it is suggested you select the 24.5 size. You may then add the 11R24.5 tire, and the savings will help you pay for the alloy wheels. Keep in mind, simply buying alloy wheels is not the only expense you will encounter. New wheel studs must be installed to accept the alloy wheels. These studs must be long enough to show about four threads after the lugs have been tightened. These longer studs, as of this writing, are about four dollars each. Multiply this times ten per wheel, times six wheels, and the added cost is over $240 plus tax, plus installation. Installation requires each brake drum be removed; have the old studs pressed or beaten out and the new studs pressed in, then reinstalled on the axle. Take a sample of your old stud when buying the new studs. There are many configurations of wheel studs in the catalog so don't simply tell the counterman you want a stud an inch longer. Take the old one to be sure you can compare the length and diameter of the seat.

For years, the suspension system of buses has been air bags. This was considered the standard of the industry until the Golden Eagle was introduced in 1958. The Eagle departed from convention by introducing the Torsilastic torsion bar suspension system. This is a suspension system which uses silicon rubber encased within a steel sleeve which maintains an almost uniform torsional resistance throughout its deflection range. For example, a conventional torsion bar increases the load resistance as it bends until the breaking point. Using the jacketed rubber torsion bar of the Torsilastic suspension, the load resistance is almost constant, ie., if it will resist 1 pound at 1 inch of twist, it will resist 1 pound at 2 inches of twist, and so forth. As the torsion bars tend to relax, they may be adjusted to bring back the original ground clearance. When all the adjustment has been made, the torsion bars may then be re-indexed, by removing them and rotating the mounting bolts over one bolt hole.

One of the drawbacks to the air bag suspension system is its lateral stability. Many of the older 96-inch wide coaches with air bags, tend to lean noticeably while going around long sweeping curves, and they are visibly affected by cross winds. In the newer coaches the air bags have been placed further outboard increasing their lateral stability immensely.

In some of the older Eagles, where the torsion bars have had all their adjustment used up, air bags have been installed over them, with the added advantage of being individually inflated for leveling purposes. Many of the older coaches use a technique of valving air to individual air bags for coach leveling purposes.

The Prevosts also use their air bags for the added advantage of being able to lift their tag axle tires for tight maneuvering or when they need more load on the drive axle.

As a final point, when working on your coach, block it up. Do not trust your suspension system, nor trust any jacking system you may have. Wooden blocks are cheap, and I have seen coaches fall off jacks. Fortunately, no one was under them when it happened.

Plumbing

Plumbing in a motor coach is virtually the same as plumbing in any location except space. The principle difference between residential plumbing and motor coach plumbing is the need to carry one's own water supply, create water pressure and have a storage for waste water.

In a residential water system, pressure is normally created through the use of a water head. This means water is stored in a location higher than its use point. For each foot of water head, the pressure increases approximately 2/5ths of a pound per square inch (0.433psi). So water in a tank at a depth of 10 feet will produce a pressure at the bottom of about 4 pounds per square inch. If this tank were elevated 100 feet in the air, it would cause a pressure at ground level of 44 psi. Just to be accurate, these figures are true at sea level.

So, how de we create water pressure in a motor coach? We can't carry a tank of water on the roof. Although I have seen this done on some *hippie buses*. The obvious answer is to use a pump to deliver water to the various use locations. This is some what akin to water delivery on a farm in Iowa where the terrain is flat and it is impractical to erect a water tower. The water is sucked up from a well and stored in a pressure tank until needed. The pressure tank creates an artificial head to produce water pressure at the tap. In our motor coach we have a pump and a hydraulic accumulator in lieu of a pressure tank. The accumulator is like a tiny pressure tank but it's principle function is to eliminate the pulsation of the pump so the water flows evenly from the spigot.

In addition to a storage tank, a pump and an accumulator to deliver fresh water,

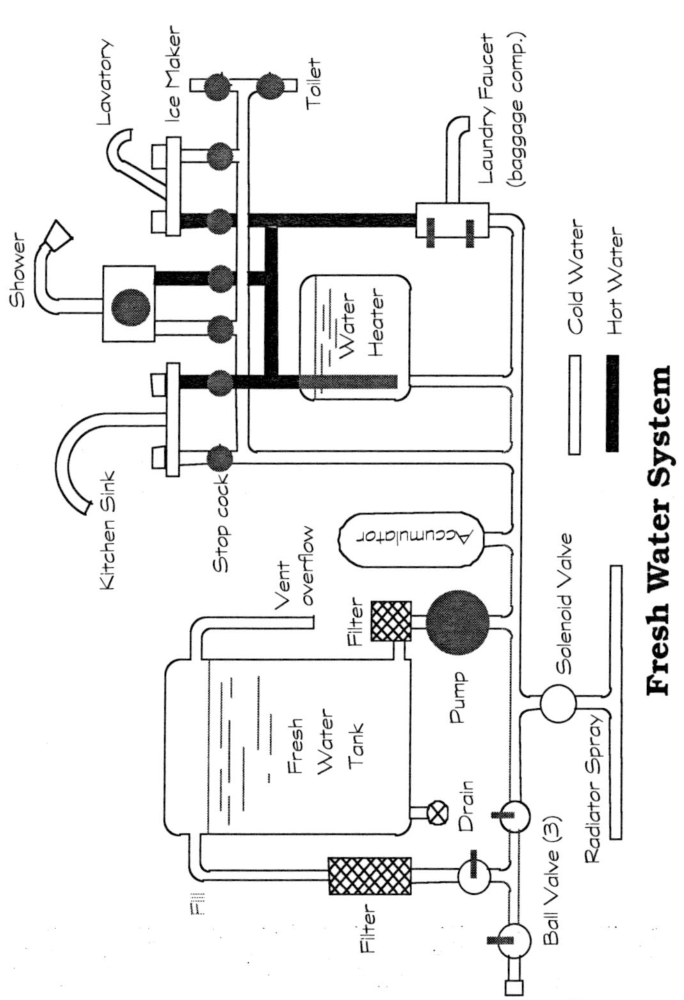

Fresh Water System

P l u m b i n g

we must have a receiver for waste water. Therefore, we have holding tanks. It is customary to have at least two holding tanks; one for grey water and one for black water. Grey water is defined as that waste water from the kitchen sink, the shower and the lavatory. Black water is the waste water from the toilet. The black water tank is normally about one-fourth to one-third the size of the grey water tank. Some systems are designed so the grey water tank drain may be attached to a hose and allowed to percolate into the ground. Due to the emphasis on environmental safety, this practice has been virtually eliminated.

Material for motor coach plumbing systems range from copper sweat fitting and pipe to plastic hand tight fittings. One of the drawbacks to copper plumbing in a motorcoach is the difficulty in adequately insulating against freezing. Plastic water pipe has the advantage of a greater tolerance to freezing than rigid metallic pipe. In addition to it's elasticity, plastic has the advantage of lower thermal conductivity, hence a better insulator.

Drain and vent piping is universally ABS plastic (acronitrile-butadiene-styrene).

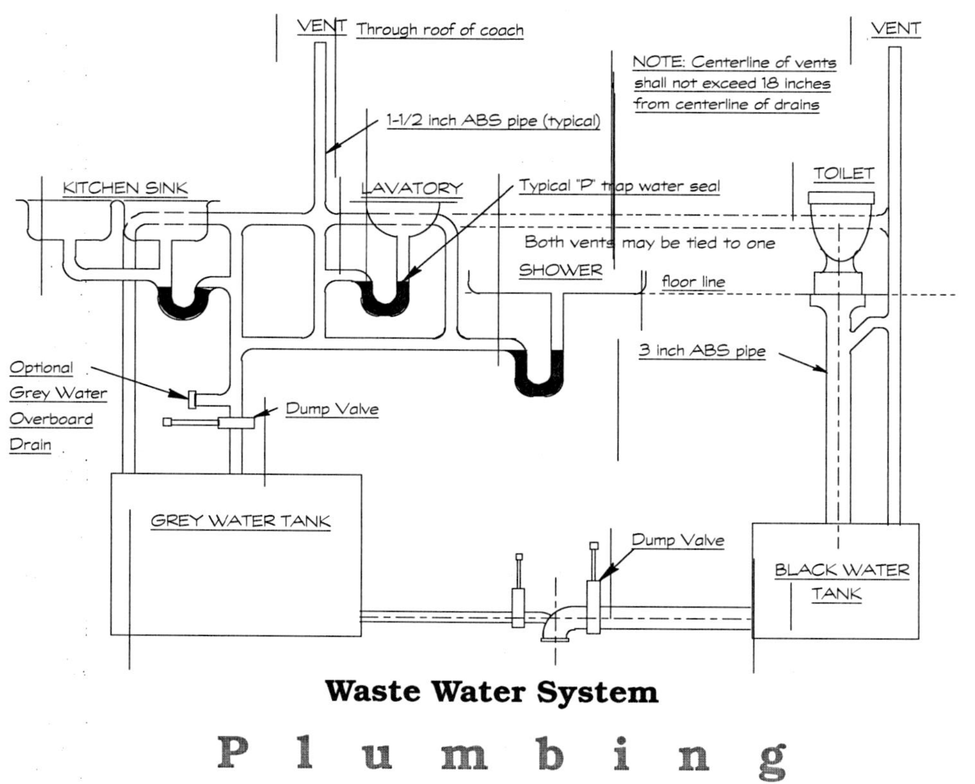

Waste Water System

P l u m b i n g

Rarely will PVC (polyvinyl chloride) be used but has been in some applications. ABS is a black flexible plastic with a long life and easily worked.

For the most part, the appliances used in a motorcoach plumbing system are equivalent to a residential installation. The single exception is the toilet. Since a flush tank toilet would work just fine in an RV, why not use it? The main reason for not installing a residential style toilet is the amount of water required for flushing. The average residential toilet uses approximately 3.6 gallons of water to flush. (In recent years Congress mandated the manufacture of toilet s using only 1.6 gallons for flushing which has led to a black market in residential toilets smuggled in from Canada. (It's funny that in the name of conservation Congress tries to repeal the laws of physics.) Regardless, a toilet design for RV use has no water trap nor a tank. It does not flush, it dumps. This dumping process is accompanied with swirling water from our fresh water pressure system to clean the bowl. Some RV toilets are made of porcelain and some are plastic. One high quality product uses vacuum to operate and is of the finest porcelain.

The diagrams shown are what we may call generic, in that they might apply to any motor coach. They are shown here for reference and may have more or less features than the average motorcoach.

Electrical Systems

The electrical system of the modern motor coach may be segregated into four separate and distinct entities. First we have the automotive system which is normally 12 volt direct current and sometimes 24 volt direct current. In almost all cases, they use a negative ground. We then have the house current which generally uses 120 volt alternating current but sometimes lighting is done with 12 volt DC. The house current may be supplied by shore power, generator, batteries, or an invertor. Finally, we have solar panels as another source of power. It is obvious, many of these various systems tend to overlap. The object of this chapter is to unravel all this overlapping and make sense of the various systems.

The common automotive system for a motorcoach consists of ignition, headlights, marker lights, turn signals, stop (brake) lights, backup lights, horn, gauges, warning lights and instrument lights. All automotive electrical systems are protected with automatic re-settable circuit breakers. A typical automotive circuit diagram is shown. Electrical Systems

1. Automotive
    a. DC Starting Batteries (12 or 24 volt)
        i. Charging
            (1) Alternator
            (2) Battery Charger
            (3) Solar Panels

2. House
    a. 120 volt AC
        i. Shore Power
            (1) Battery Charger

(a) House batteries

ii. Generator

(1) Battery charger

(a) House Batteries

iii. Invertor

(1) Sub Panel

b. 12 volt DC

i. Charging

(1) Solar Panels

(2) Invertor

(3) Alternator

ii House lighting

House Power

No, this is not a misspelling of *Horsepower*. House power is the electrical system used to provide power to the living quarters of our motor coaches. Power sources are: 1) Batteries, 2) Generator, 3) Shore hookup, and 4) Solar panels. Wind driven generators are another possible source but are rarely used on a motor coach. Another possible source is an engine driven 120 volt alternator. I have not seen these applied to motor coaches although they are a common source of power in ambulances.

The batteries give us direct current and we can often convert that direct current directly into illumination. Occasionally, direct current can be converted directly into heating, but at a high cost in amperes. To run normal residential electrical appliances, we must convert the direct current from batteries into alternating current and at a high voltage. This is where the neat little gadget called an invertor jumps into the system.

The modern invertor with it's modified square wave and high power capacity, can convert battery power into enough power to comfortably operate a microwave oven, a toaster, a hair dryer, a VCR, a stereo and several televisions sets. All of this , of course, within the amp-hour capacity of the battery bank.

The house batteries are normally deep cycle which means they may be discharged and charged many times before they fail. Golf cart batteries are designed for deep cycle use. A standard automobile battery is designed for high ampere starting current but will not normally take very many charge and discharge cycles.

Deep cycle batteries are rated in amp-hours. This gives an indication of it's usage before it has to be recharged. A 100 amp-hour battery should last for 100 hours at a one amp load, or 10 hours at a 10 amp load, or 1 hour at a 100 amp load. It is common practice to use only one-half of the total rated amp-hours before planning to recharge. An example of amp-hour usage might be as follows:

Make toast: 1200 watt / 12 volts x 1/10 hour (6 minutes) = 10 amp-hours (AH)

Television : 120 watt / 12 volts x 2 hours = 20 amp-hours

Microwave Oven: 1200 watt/ 12 volts x 1/30 hour (2 minutes) = 3.33 amp-hours

I have seen some coaches with as many as 10 deep cycles batteries adding up to over 2,000 amp-hour capacity. Often, this type of coach is an all electric motorhome. This includes electric cooking but not normally electric heating. Heating in this type of coach is a diesel fired boiler. An average motor coach will have at least 400 to 600 amp-hours of battery capacity. This may be achieved with four-120 AH batteries.

An average day one might use 10 AH for coffee, 10 AH for toast, 10 AH for Microwave and 30 AH for TV or Stereo. This adds up to about 60 AH per day. If the coach has a capacity of 480 AH, then using only half that capacity for a safety margin, one could reasonably dry camp for four days before worrying about recharging the battery bank. On the other hand, if air conditioning were needed, the generator would have to supply power, since battery power would be inadequate.

Keep in mind, invertors are not 100 percent efficient. We will expect some loss depending on the load. For example, a small load will experience a greater percentage of inefficiency than a large load. In other words, it takes more overhead proportionally to create a low wattage load than it does a higher wattage load. Imagine a motor generator producing a 120 volt alternating current. Before the days of the solid state invertor, this was the common device used to convert DC power to AC power. The most common unit was the Honeywell ReadyLine, or PowerLine (trade marks of the Honeywell Company). These units had a DC motor connected to an AC generator. On demand, they would spin up to a specific rpm and AC power could be extracted. It cost a minimum of approximately 10 amps overhead simply to rotate the motor. So, if one was only operating a small load, such as a television, the efficiency factor was about 55 percent. However, if a large load, such as a coffee maker, were on, the efficiency could go up to about 80 percent. Today's modern solid state invertors can maintain an efficiency rating somewhere between 90 and 97 percent. This means you get more bang for your buck, or you might say, more usable amps per charge.

Generators

by Dick Wright

Believe it or not, the average 200 amp residential service is provided by a 10,000 watt (10 KW) transformer. Now, I know that doesn't compute. 200 amps at 120 volts is 24 kilowatts. The reason I know this is true, is a tornado ripped out about a mile and a half of power lines along the street in front of our house. When the power company re-erected the power poles, they hung only a 10 KW transformer to convert the 24000 volts to 240 volt for my house. Being a smart-alecky engineer, I challenged them, declaring we had 200 amp service and we needed a 24 KW transformer. I was informed, that if the 10 KW did not do the job they would install a bigger one. Well, it's been ten years and we have not had a problem. These transformers are oil cooled and capable of large surge loads for a long period of time.

The size of the generator should be large enough to satisfy the demands of every appliance in the coach including their start-up load factor. Start-up load factors are not relevant in heating type devices such as lamps, heaters and televisions. Start-up factors should be considered with any type of rotating machinery, such as motors and air conditioners. Although these factors vary with the type of motor and the load conditions, it is important to use a load factor ranging from 5 to 7 on these applications. Even the modern rotary air conditioners with a running load of 15 amps need about 80 amps to start.

Generators may be set to provide either 240-volt alternating current (AC), or 120-volt AC. This is a preference to be made by the owner. By selecting the 240VAC option, two 120-volt legs may be run to the distribution panel, but the problem of balancing the loads must be solved. The advantages of the 240-volt option is one leg may be dedicated to relatively small loads for convenience, such as lighting and entertainment. This leg may then also be supplied by an inverter powered by the battery bank to provide electrical conveniences while the generator is not running. In balancing the load with a 240-volt system, it is obvious if two air conditioning units are used, each one should be supplied by each leg. One drawback with the inverter dedicated to one leg and an air conditioner also running on that leg is, if the generator were to shut down, the inverter would try to run the Air Conditioner (A/C) depleting the batteries and damaging the A/C. Other high load appliances should be as evenly shared by the two legs as possible. Another advantage to the 240-volt system, is the capability of operating high voltage equipment, such as an electric cook-top, or a welder directly from the generator. 120 VAC cooktops and welders, however, are available. As far as hooking up to shore power where only low voltage is available, the land line, or umbilical simply plugs into an adapter feeding both legs with a single hot lead. These adapters are available in RV supply stores. However, it must be cautioned, with this system 240-volt appliances could not be operated. In order to design for 240-volt appliances, a hot lead is employed from each leg, and the shore line must be plugged into a 240-volt source, a convenience not available in every trailer park.

Without a doubt, the simplest way to set up the generator is 120-volt AC. With this approach, there is no need to balance the load distribution. The inverter(s) may then serve a selected group of appliances through a sub-panel. The battery bank delivering power to the inverter, however, must be capable of supplying all the electrical demands of this sub panel. If the battery bank is too small to achieve these demands, it is mandatory the inverter be able to be switched out of the system in the event the generator is providing power, but fails for some reason. If this were to happen, the battery bank would be depleted in short order.

Generators are available in gasoline, propane, or diesel power. Since our conversions are primarily powered with diesel fuel, it is logical to select a diesel powered generator. Many conversions do use both diesel and propane. Although propane does not have the efficiency that diesel fuel has, it is an extremely clean burning fuel. In addition, propane fueled motors remain exceptionally clean.

If a diesel fueled generator is selected because it is the common fuel of the primary coach engine, it is important not to simply "tee-off" from the coach fuel line. The coach engine pump moves well over sixty gallons of fuel per hour. This would probably starve the generator if an attempt were made to run them simultaneously. So, it is imperative a separate fuel line and return fuel line be dedicated to the generator.

The generator should be mounted in a clean compartment with a flow of fresh air available. This fresh air may be achieved by installing a blower or fan. The radiator for the generator may be remotely mounted, as long as it too has a supply of clean, fresh, cool air. For example, it would not be wise to mount the generator radiator in the coach engine compartment where it would be subject to the hot air radiating from the motor. A logical location would be a baggage compartment behind the forward axle bulkhead, where a source of cooling air may be obtained between the steering tires. Another common acceptable practice is to connect the generator cooling system into the coach cooling system. This has the advantage in that the coach engine temperature gauges also reflect the temperature of the generator engine.

It is recommended the generator be mounted in a frame or cage which may be rolled out or swung out in order to simplify maintenance, although some generators may be serviced from only one side. It is recommended the exhaust from the generator be directed to a remote location while parked next to other coaches. An ideal solution would be to direct the exhaust through the roof of the coach. This may be done by routing the exhaust pipe through a slightly larger section of transite, cement pipe, or other form of insulating conduit.

A small editorial note might be appropriate at this point. Commonly we hear house voltage referred to as 110 volts, or 115 volts, or even 117 volts. And, we often hear the higher voltage referred to as 220. Voltage is derived as a result of the division of the transmission of very high voltage. Although the value of the transmitted voltage varies according to the distance and the terrain, one of the more common transmission voltages is 12,000 volts. Step down transformers are then employed to divide this transmitted voltage down to 480 volts, and 240 volts. Almost all voltage delivered to a residence through a step down transformer is 240 volts. Appliance makers often refer to a design operating voltage of 117. This is to compensate for voltage drops as a result of normal line loss due to conductor resistance. At anytime, a meter may be applied to a wall outlet in a house and the voltage will fluctuate from about 108 on the low side to as high as 124. These fluctuations are caused by a myriad of reasons, from public demand to sun spots. As is obvious from the discussion above, I prefer to stick to the simplicity of multiples of 120. The principle advantage this has, it is easily divisible by the most common direct current voltage, ie., 12 and 24 volts.

One very important accessory for the generator should be considered. This is an automatic start device that may be added for about ten percent additional cost to the generator. This automatic start system may be triggered by several options. One option built into the system, is a low battery condition. This will sense a low battery bank, turn on your generator, recharge your batteries to a specific level, then shut itself off. The low battery sensor is designed to sample your voltage over a time period so it will not start the generator simply because of a transitory condition. Another form of sensor, samples the outside temperature. This sensor may be set for a low temperature so your generator may turn on and drive electric heaters to warm your coach, or to sense a high temperature so that your air conditioning may be powered on automatically. Obviously, manual controls are built in so you may turn off this feature if you don't want it operable while you are sleeping. This accessory has a built in alarm buzzer warning anyone in near proximity it is about to start. Finally, the number of start attempts may be adjusted, since sometimes motors do not always start on the first try. This can be set for maximum reliability.

GENERATOR COURTESY

You are dry camping at a gathering of other coaches, a rally. You have an all electric coach so you must run your generator frequently. We are not aware of the convenience of the Edison company until we are in this situation. First, generators are noisy and second, they stink! A proper installation will address both these conditions. Adequate sound insulation will mitigate much of the annoying noise level. Proper exhaust installation will help the second problem.

Once we were parked in a group of several thousand coaches where it was impossible to relocate. The people in the coach next to us ran their generator continuously for the several days of the convention. To compound matters, their exhaust was pointed at our bedroom window and they had no sound insulation. I tried to reason with them, but I was informed they had to run their generator to make oxygen for one of the occupants suffering from emphysema. Obviously, they were unaware they were sharing this illness with their neighbors.

Generators should not be started before 7:00 AM and should always be shut down by 11:00 PM. This practice has become an adopted convention throughout the RV community. Even in a coach which is all electric, this procedure can be achieved, since all totally electric coaches have adequate battery banks to carry them through their periods of disconnection.

Editor's Note:

Dick Wright owns WRICO International from Eugene, Oregon, manufacturers of diesel powered generators for motor coaches. He has been involved with motor coaching for over 20 years and has served as president of the Northwest Bus Nuts, a chapter of FMCA.

Converters, Inverters, and Chargers

A converter is basically a device which converts alternating current, like standard residential current to direct current through a *rectifier*. A *rectifier* is basically a large step down transformer with diodes, or electrical check valves which force the alternating current to emerge as a directional one way current. This permits the converter to act like a battery charger. In addition, a converter will have a series of fuse holders so a direct current system of circuits may be distributed throughout the coach. Converters are not as often seen with the advance of solid state devices.

An inverter is an electrical device which does the opposite of a converter. It takes direct current and changes it to alternating current, such as we have in our houses. The earlier inverters were direct current motors driving an alternator. The most common unit was made by Honeywell, known as a Readyline. Readyline, and Powerline are trademarks of Honeywell. These units were available in 500, 1000 and 1500 watts. No doubt, larger sizes were available, but not as common. The principle problem with the motor driven inverters was the high overhead in battery power needed to operate them. For example, a 1000-watt unit could run a television which used only 120 watts. But instead of drawing 10 amps from the battery bank, it would draw over 15 amps. This was because a minimum power drain was used to simply turn the rotor. This results in a poor efficiency rating for the rotating style of the inverter; on the order of 55 to 70 percent. Additionally, the rotating inverter has a whine which can get on your nerves if you are sensitive to noise. These are quite a few drawbacks, but in the earlier days, it was the only game in town.

The solid state inverter has been around for a number of years, but the earlier ones also had a relatively poor efficiency rating. Tripp is a brand name which comes to mind. The earlier solid state inverters also had an annoying hum, or buzz. In recent years, we have seen the development of the computerized solid state inverters with no moving parts. These units are made by Trace, Best, Heart and no doubt, others. These companies have most aggressively entered the RV market. The units are commonly available in 2,000, 2,500, and 5,000 watts. For greater power requirements they may be stacked, or cascaded. This means they may be installed so that their power capabilities are added together to provide all the power a coach needs. In addition, a common inverter option is a built-in battery charger. With the addition of a simple fuse holder for direct current applications, the need for a converter disappears. Another option instead of a fuse holder, is a bank of re-settable circuit breakers for direct current applications. Inverters have other options such as remote readout panels, and remote on/off controls. The readout panels will display such information as the battery voltage, charging rate in amps, the peak to peak input voltage, and the frequency of the alternating current. The frequency readout feature is especially useful when setting the speed of the generator drive engine, in the event you receive your generator in an uncalibrated condition or in case the generator motor has to be repaired.

Battery chargers are an essential piece of equipment. They are simply a source of direct current connected in parallel with the battery system. A battery charger is generally set to provide a direct current at 13.8 volts. This value permits the batteries to recharge, but not boil out the battery acid. In many respects storage batteries may be equated to pails of power, similar to buckets of water. If two batteries were placed side by side with different charges and were connected, the higher charge would pour over into the lesser charge. After a time their charges would be equal. This is similar to *water seeking its own level.* In a simplified manner, this is basically what a battery charger does. A bank of batteries whose reading may be 12.3 volts, when connected to a 13.8 volt charging system will, ultimately, come up to 13.8 volts over a period of time. The charger will begin by charging at a high rate, but will, as the voltage builds up in the batteries, taper down to a trickle, hence the term *trickle charge.*

A very sophisticated form of charger is now available for a fairly high cost. This is a marine pulse charger. A unit rated at only 20 amps can cost over $400. A pulse charger is a unique concept in that it has been determined a storage battery would prefer to accept replenishing charges in small doses, instead of a continuous flow. These pulse chargers have been known to restore a depleted battery which has been judged ready for the scrap heap.

Another interesting form of battery charger is the photovoltaic cell or group of cells known as solar panels. This is the passive charging system . Many of us are familiar with the LED (light emitting diode), a small device that lights up when a voltage is impressed across it. The photovoltaic cell is the opposite of the LED. If a light is shone on the photovoltaic cell, it will yield a voltage. A large array of these cells are combined together to form a solar panel. Solar panels are available in many voltages and power combinations. In the very early days of the solar panel, they were selling for about three dollars per watt; very expensive even by today's standard. It was predicted then the price of the solar panel would ultimately descend to about thirty cents a watt. Because of manufacturing difficulties and a monopoly, this never happened and the price of solar panels is still quite high. For approximately 400 plus dollars, however, solar panels may be mounted on the roof of a conversion to provide a battery charging capability from the sun, or even a street lamp. Since many of the solar panels are designed to put out about 18 volts, a voltage regulator is necessary. The voltage of a solar panel is not a constant thing because of the varying intensity of the impinging light. Obviously, on a bright sunny day with the sun nearly overhead, more voltage will be generated than on a dull overcast day with the late afternoon sun.

Wind generators have been available for many years, but I know of no practical unit available for the RV industry. I recall a small wind driven generator to light a lamp on my bicycle which I had as a kid.

Finally, the most common form of battery charger is the motor driven alternator mounted on the primary engine. The more modern units have built-in regulator/ rectifying diodes so a voltage regulator is becoming a thing of the past. These are used primarily to maintain the starting batteries voltage, and provide power for the lighting, and automotive accessories. However, a simple circuit shown on page 270 is designed so the alternator charges the house batteries as you travel down the road.

Electrical Circuits

The diagram shown on page 270 is typical of the electrical system of the modern motor coach. The dotted lines represent alternating current and the solid lines depict direct current.

The change-over box may be either an automatic system actuated by heavy duty relays, or a manual system consisting of a rotary or knife switch. The change-over box receives power from either the generator or a shore power hookup and delivers it to the main panel. The main panel provides power to the complete coach, plus a battery charger and a sub panel. The sub panel will provide service only to those circuits capable of being powered by the invertor. As an example: if a heater circuit were supplied by the invertor, the battery bank would be depleted in short order, so the sub panel would not service such a circuit.

Although the battery charger and the invertor are shown as separate units, they may be combined into a single unit. As may be seen by the diagram, solar panels are optional.

The purpose of the two switches are to tie both the starting batteries and the house batteries together when one or the other are being charged. SW 2 may be closed by engine oil pressure to couple the two batteries when the motor is running. This allows the alternator to charge both the engine batteries and the house batteries. When plugged into shore power or power supplied by the generator, SW 1 may be closed by a 120 volt AC relay. This now permits the battery charger to charge the starting batteries as well. The solar panels are passive and will charge only the house batteries when neither the motor is running or AC power is absent.

Some very sophisticated coaches have banks of switches located strategically which will operate every lamp or system. Such locations are the entry door, the bathroom, the bedroom, the living room and the cockpit. This permits one to switch on all the lights from the entry and later switch all the lights off from the bedroom while arming a security system. Systems such as these require many relays and miles of signal wire. Other methods make use of remote signaling devices such as a television remote control. One inexpensive system, sold by Radio Shack, uses receivers which may be plugged into a convenience outlets, with the appliances, in turn, connected to the receivers. The remote control is portable and may be moved about the coach. Multiple remote control units may be placed about the coach for convenience.

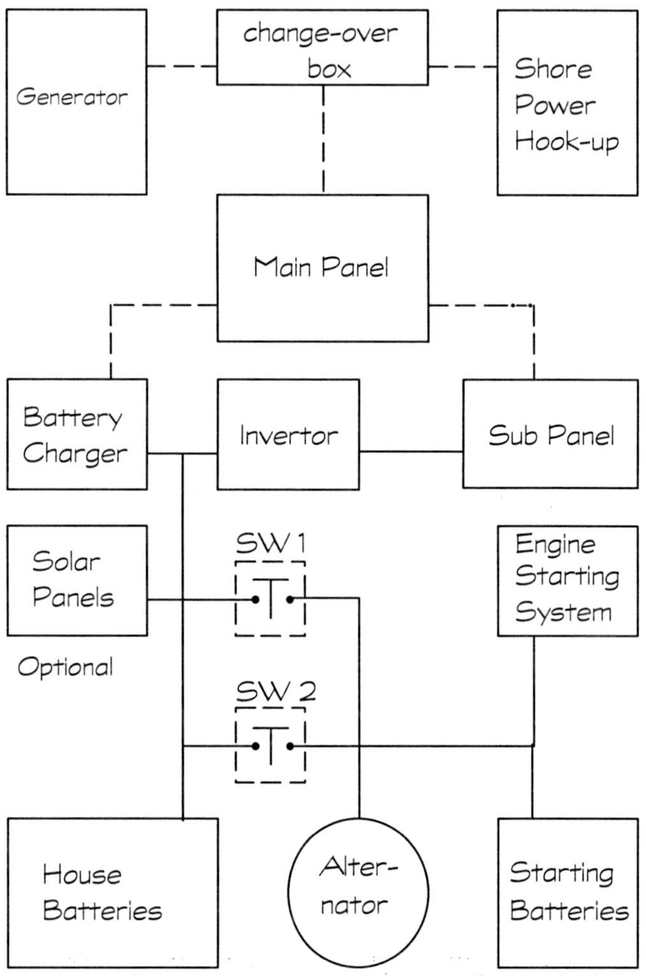

SW1= 120VAC relay to charge starting batteries when generator, or shore power in use.
SW2 = 12 VDC relay, ignition actuated, to charge house batteries when under way.

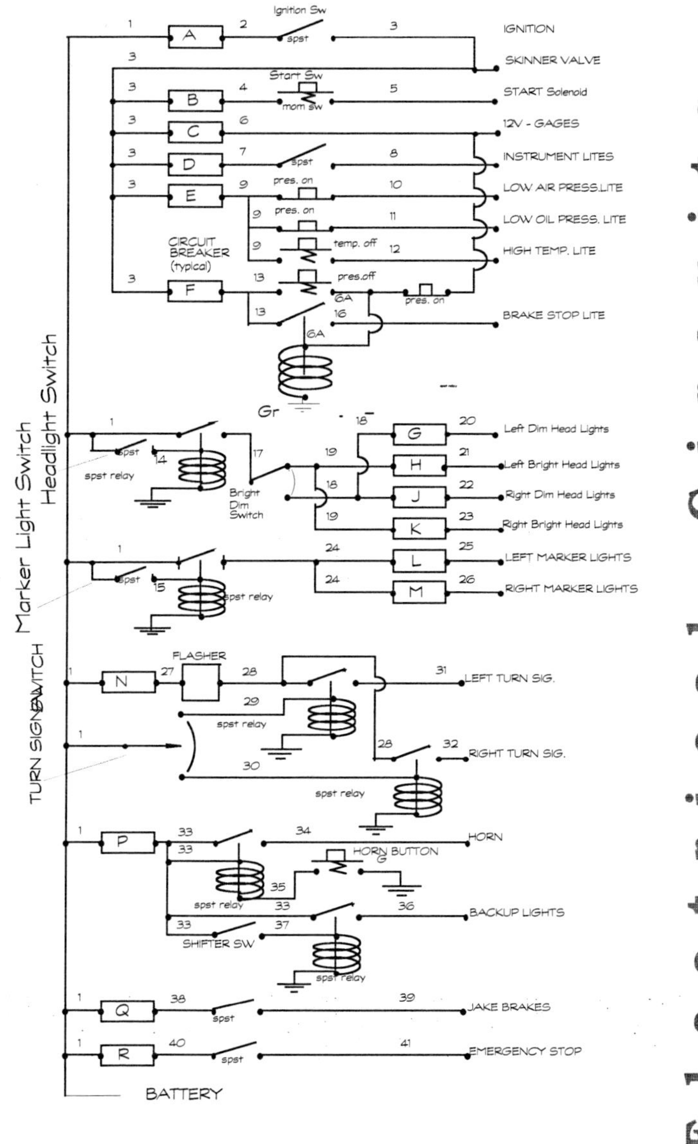

Electrical Circuits

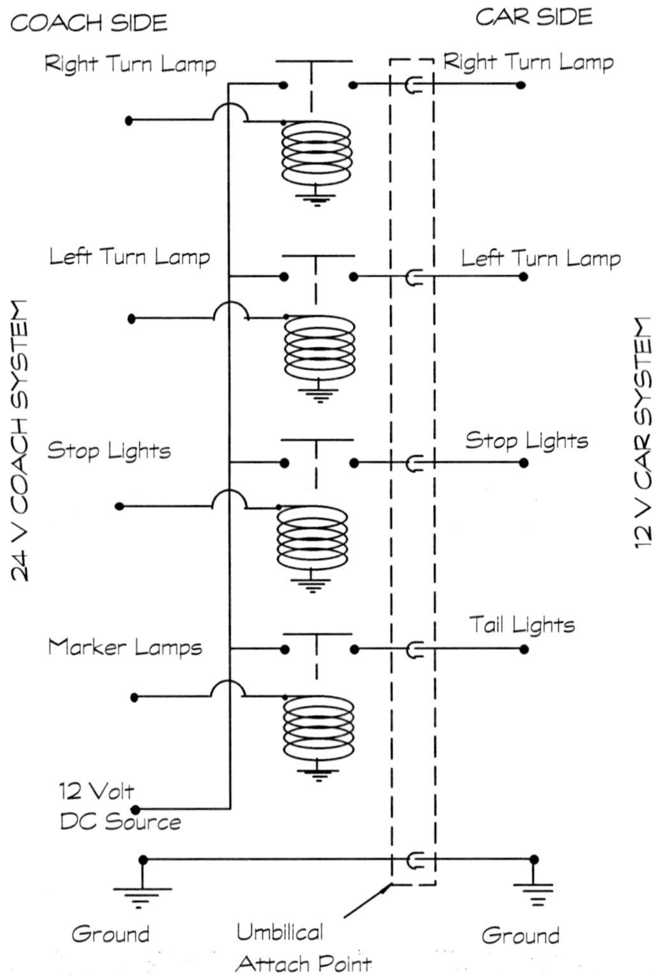

24 V TO 12 V INTERFACE
(for 24 V Coaches)

Radio Communications

"Breaker, breaker, This is Lug Nut on nineteen southbound. Any bears out today?" "Lug Nut, this is Rachet Jaw. Bear got 'im a four wheeler at seventy-three." "Ten Fo, Ah Appree-cee-ate-tit!" Translation" Anyone listening on channel 19, this is a trucker heading south. Are there any highway patrols south of me?" "This is another trucker heading north. There is a highway patrol officer ticketing a car at mile marker 73." "I understand, thank you."

All of us have a CB radio but not all of

us use it very often. This is a very useful tool when en-route. We can listen to the truckers on channels 19 and 21 and learn of road conditions and where the *Bears* are. Additionally, channel 9 is an emergency channel, which should be used to call for help in an emergency. My personal experience with channel 9 has been pretty poor, though. Once in Florida we came on an accident and used our CB on channel 9 to call for help. No one responded so I got on channel 19 and got some response.

When we are traveling in caravan with another group of motor coaches, the CB is busy all the time. Sometimes it is so busy we can't get a word into the conversation. The neat thing is, if we are traveling with five or six other rigs, we can all agree on a stopping place for lunch or a whiz stop and a sight seeing excursion. There will always be a *Hot Dog* who wants to do his own thing, but it is a great way to stay in contact.

Almost any brand of Citizens Band Radio will work. There are a number of models for each brand with more bells and whistles but a basic CB radio is all one needs. Linear amplifiers on the order of 100 to 200 watts can be had but all they do is distort your signal up close. The most important item with any transmitting radio is the antenna. The antenna must be tuned so it's standing -wave ratio is at a minimum.

The average maximum range of a good CB installation is about 2 to 3 miles. With a linear amplifier you can extend that range but when you transmit to someone within a normal range, your signal is so distorted as to become unintelligible. Back in my early days, I believed everything anyone would tell me and I had to get *Twin Trucker* antennas. This is a pair of antennas which mount on each side of the coach. For a big rig, the purpose is to avoid a shadow created by the trailer being towed by the semi-truck. Well, on a motor coach, it was kind of dumb, but I have some fond memories of those *twin truckers*.

A number of years ago we traveled deep into Mexico with the Meximaniac Twelve. This was a caravan of 12 coaches who decided to explore Mexico, and gave themselves the aforementioned name. I experienced an antenna problem that may bear repeating. We had just entered the beautiful city of Hermosillo. At that time when you drove south it was necessary to pass through the heart of this city. Today I believe that they have built a bypass so that you may miss the heart of the town.

As we were going through Hermosillo we drove down a beautiful two-lane divided boulevard with a center divider sporting shrubbery and, on the curb side, low growing trees. Naturally our speed was quite slow so we could enjoy the beauty while being careful of the traffic. Furthermore, we felt compelled to occupy the inside lane since it appeared that the trees on the curb side were too low for our coaches.

Throughout the trip we kept a fairly constant flow of communication with our CB radios. We were nearly halfway through the city when I heard an unfamiliar voice on the CB radio declare, "There is an accident up ahead. We should all move to the outside lane." So without questioning the source, I immediately moved into the outside lane.

I heard a noise or two as we traveled this outside lane. I could only assume that the low growing trees were catching on my CB antenna. You see, I was the proud possessor of *Twin-Trucker* CB antennas, one on each side of the bus. We never did come upon the forewarned accident.

Later, after we had cleared the city, we stopped for a walk-around break. I decided to inspect my antenna on the right side to see if the trees had caused any damage. As I looked up at my antenna, I was looking at nothing. It was not there where it belonged. Some damned Mexican tree ate it! Oh well, I still had the one on the left side of the bus and I could still transmit and receive O.K.

We continued on that day and spent the night at the Rio Fuerte Trailer Park in Los Moches by the river of the same name. Rio Fuerte may be translated *Strong River*. The next day we arrived at Mazatlan.

We drove up to the *La Posta* trailer park in Mazatlan and stopped outside. Then we all went in to register. One by one as we were registered, we drove around back to find our spots. While driving down the narrow drive to get to the back of the park where our spaces were, I heard another twang. Again I figured I may have been too close to the trees on the left side of us this time.

I parked the coach and went around to see if any damage had been done to the left side of the bus. Damn! No antenna on that side now! Fortunately I was able to walk back along the path I had just driven and locate my errant antenna. I was able to repair and reinstall it on the driver's side.

Somehow, Mexican trees had really developed a taste for my CB antennas.

Where Am I?

I love maps. When I was taught to read maps in the army I had discovered a fun new game. I could look out at the terrain and find the features on our maps. And, with the lensatic compass I had a toy that would always provide an endless source of entertainment. So much for my military testimonial.

Remember when you could pull into any service station, (or filling station, as we used to call them) and you could get all the maps you needed, FREE!. Man, that has gone the way of the nickel hamburger! Now if you need a map, you pick one up in a stationary store or a truck stop for a buck or two. Don't despair, there are still some freebies though. Almost, every state you enter has a *visitors information center.* And, almost every one of these will give you a free map of their state.

We are not talking about a tactical map, or a topographical map. We are concerned with a road map showing all the Interstate highways and the red and blue highways. These maps always fold up into a nice neat package which can never be duplicated. They always have tiny numbers printed between cities and town showing mileage from one little pointy thing to another little pointy thing. It's always a little confusing as to which little pointy thing some of these number refer to.

One other area of confusion is that the country is now converting to the metric system. This means if you want to know how far something is and it is listed in kilometers, you have to multiply by 1.625 to learn it's real distance. The metric system is terribly confusing since it is based on the number ten. Starting with a millimeter which is about forty-thousandths of an inch, we progress to a centimeter, about as thick as your thumb, to a meter, a little longer than a yardstick ,and finally to a kilometer which is about two-thirds of a mile.

I grew up learning that 12 blocks was a mile and a foot was about as long as your foot and an inch was the length of your first thumb joint. How sensible can you get? I guess I'll forever be converting metric dimensions to real numbers.

Returning to our discussion of maps, the easiest way to have maps is to buy a book, or an atlas. The other option is to stop at the visitors information kiosk at every state and pick up a free map. I have done both and have a nice box of maps I'll probably never use again. But, then, there is pride of ownership. I use up an Atlas about every four or five years, but they are only about ten bucks, and I'm worth it!

If you happen to belong to the American Automobile Association, (AAA), you can get all the free maps you want (within reason). Another neat thing they do, is make up strip maps for you. These are a few inches wide and contain only the highway you told them you wanted to use.

Of course, they will send you in a direction they think is best. It is kind of like a tunnel vision sort of map. Don't go off of it or you may get lost and may have a hard time finding your way back onto the strip.

In this day and age of magic in the form of computers, and more importantly the laptop computer, we now have all sorts of software to plan our trips. I've bought 'em all. There is TripMaker by Rand McNally, AutoMap by Microsoft and Map-N-Go by Delorme. My favorite computer mapping software, however, is Street Atlas, USA by Delorme. In addition to this software which can take you to almost any address in the country, a little GPS receiver can be attached to your computer and the program will locate your position on the map. It does have it's failing however: it is accurate to only a few yards (or meters.)

Perhaps the most well known GPS device for the motor vehicle is the Street Pilot by Garmin. This unit sells for around $500 and individual map inserts are available for various cities for about $100 to $200 depending upon the city and it's complexity. Garmin has been marketing GPS units for years and their products are made principally for fishermen, flyers and off road enthusiasts.

Delorme's GPS receiver is called TripMate and a newer version has come out called EarthMate. They both do the same thing, that is, locate you position on the surface of our globe by triangulating from a series of stationary satellites. The satellites are known as Global Positioning Satellites, hence, GPS. Many GPS receivers are available but most of them are designed for ship or boat navigation and a lot are designed for the outback hiker and camper. The most recognized brand name is Magellan and many of them are hand held so the rugged outdoors man can find his way to his stash of beer.

The little GPS receiver by Delorme can be simply set on the dash board of our vehicle and, even though many of our windshield are almost vertical, it will pick up several satellite signals. I was totally amused one time to discover when I had pulled into a rest stop, the transponder had shown we were slightly off the super slab parked in a rest stop. How else would we have known that? OK, this is kind of dumb, but it's a new toy and it's a lot of fun

Remember when we had to find a filling station or a rest stop to make a telephone call? Well, now all we have to do is pick up our cellular phone and call anyone we want for only about $25 per minute. In a few years, even this is going to change, Next we will all have our PCS phone. Personal Communication Service is only about a year away from this writing. This is a telephone system when you will be assigned a number and it will stay with you anywhere you go. You can call from Hawaii or New York or London and it's a local call. It will all be relayed via satellite. There is no guarantee a local call via PCS will be a dime a minute, but it may be close.

Next, we will discuss the WWW, World Wide Web. Is it a time waster or a boon? I have prevailed on a friend of mine who is also a motor coaching nut to discuss computers and the internet. In the next chapter, please meet Ian Giffin, the Bossnut of the Busnuts.

Editor's Note: It has just been brought to my attention that I failed to mention the Lowrance GlobalMap 1600, another GPS unit. I apologize to all the other GPS manufacturers if I left them out. -

THE PLAIN ENGLISH GUIDE TO ACCESSING THE WORLD WIDE WEB

Ian Giffin

Computers

The word either piques your curiosity or makes you want to run away from your grandchildren's room screaming.

I suggested to Dave (the editor) that he make this chapter of his book a pullout section for those who fall into the latter category. If, as you hold this book, you are a member of the computer resistive (new computer term, invented for this book) and this chapter does, indeed, detach from the rest of this book, feel free to dispose of this section in the fireplace (but, please, keep the rest of the book!).

However, if I have been able to retain your attention, thus far, please reread this chapter's title. If you are expecting words like Pentium, Hypertext, Dial-up or Javascript to appear, please do not fret! Here, you will find the layman's version of everything you'll need to know about computing and accessing the Internet.

Take a deep breath; this won't hurt a bit... here we go!

The first thing we shall cover is the computer itself. In order to access the world's largest library - the Internet - you will need to have a computer. Instead of getting technical here by stating that you need a Pentium II MMX-400-Celeron with 128 MEG of RAM, dual exhaust and blah, blah, blah, suffice it to say that if you go into your local computer superstore and ask for a good quality multimedia computer and spend between $1,000. and $1,500, you will walk away with a decent computer that is ready for the Internet.

There are small portable computers, called laptops, that you may want to consider, which cost about twice as much as the home style, or desktop, computer. These computers will also play your audio CD's, keep a handy telephone directory, save all your recipes without getting food stains all over them, detail a complete maintenance log of your RV, store your complete traveling memoirs and calculate your taxes at the end of the year. This chapter pertains only to the retrieval of information from the Internet.

You may wonder why you would want to access the world's largest library? Good question! Just imagine you are sitting at home one night entertaining and one of your know-it-all-done-it-all-friends (and we all have one of those, don't we?) is regaling the assembled crowd with one of his/her many unbelievable stories. You are now able to immediately jump onto the Internet and determine the authenticity of your blow-hard friend's story and, therefore, empowered to discredit or support him/her, finally shutting them, or you, up forever. What a perk!

This, alone may be worth many times the cost of a new computer.

Try this little self-test: While you're watching TV some night, pay particular attention to the commercials. Almost every one of them makes reference to their Internet web site. The format you will most likely see is www.something.com. Your favorite magazine will also have many of these same references. What the advertisers are giving you is an address; an Internet address, called a URL (Uniform Resource Locator - the standard World Wide Web address format, e.g. http://www.something.com). Books in a library have addresses, too. Now, imagine looking in a library for a book with a specific topic, e.g. bus conversions, and when you find the book that interests you, you find that it also contains thousands upon thousands of cross referenced topics. Imagine then, that the same book would automatically skip to the next topic of interest at your command. Imagine doing that many hundreds of times without ever having to put the first book down to pick up another. That's what the Internet is. The Internet is not only for advertisers; it has topics of interest for every imaginable topic that you can think of. If you can't think of one, it will even help you find one.

What is the Internet? The Internet is a bunch of computers that are connected to each other. They contain all the information (in various addresses, as mentioned above) which people have put there for others to access via their own computers. I'll attempt to portray a simple image of what I mean: Picture a globe with an outer skin hovering above the earth's surface. The skin is made up of all the information available on the Internet. Picture it as a physical entity. Picture your computer as having a probe that sticks up into the sky, penetrating into this skin becoming a part of the "network" of computers. As part of the network of computers, you now have access to any information you wish, made available to you from all the other computers.

How does it all work together? You have heard the Internet referred to as "the information highway." In reality, this is a very close analogy! Information travels literally both directions on this "highway." I'll explain this in two short sentences:

1. Information **providers** transfer the information they have to a local computer

Internet company who, in turn, connects to many computers which, together, make up the Internet backbone or network.

2. Internet **users** (you, in this case) connect to the Internet through a telephone line (or more recently, cable television lines) which has access to all the computers on the Internet network or highway.

Of course, this all costs a lot of money to maintain. However, even that is simple to explain. You pay a small fee to access the Internet through your service provider (explained in the next paragraph). Information providers pay a small fee to send information to the network and maintain the information there. These small fees add up: At the beginning of 1999, there will be well over 100 million Internet connections. That's why the World Wide Web has become big business!

See? Not as mysterious as you thought!!

Just a note to let you know that the Internet and how it works is far more complicated than I have shown here. My sincere apologies to web professionals, worldwide, who have suffered heart failure as a result of reading my oversimplified renderings.

How to connect? Easy. In the area you live, there are likely several Internet Service Providers (ISP's). To locate one, simply go to a local computer store and ask who the best ISP in the area is. Most locales will give you two or three choices. Large cities will likely have dozens to chose from. If the choices are too many for you to make an informed decision, ask a neighbor, friend or relative for their recommendations.

We'll skip over the part where you need to get all the stuff in your computer working together to make the connection to the Internet. This writer presumes that if you experience any difficulty in the setup of your computer, it's operating system, the various programs to run on the computer or any other aspect of computer operations, that you will seek the professional services of a local computer shop to get you going. Or ask one of your kids!

Where do you go from here? At this point, the author presupposes that you have your computer, that you have selected an Internet Service Provider and that you are now connected to the Internet.

Browsers - what are they? A browser

is a template screen on your computer which allows you to view Internet web sites through the integration of text and images; the gateway, as it were, to the Internet. Two browsers make up about 90% of the total browser usage - they are Netscape and Internet Explorer. Either of these browsers will display any web page you wish to peruse.

What do you do about that blank browser screen? Easy... in the "Location" bar of the browser, type in a topic you are interested in - don't forget to press the [Enter] button! I'll give you "bus conversions" as an example (don't include the quotation marks). The latest browser software automatically conducts a search of the entire Internet using your search parameters (bus conversions). After a moment, if your computer has a dumb stare on it's face, you probably have an older browser version. Type in "yahoo" (without the quotes) and wait for the screen to give you a result.

Yahoo (aptly named because one tends to shout this word out loud when one finally finds the specific topic they were looking for) is an Internet search engine that searches for inputted words based on suggestions from the owner of a particular web site. In other words, a web site owner who is providing information about oranges will submit the word "oranges" to the Yahoo web site. When you type in "oranges" into the search location, that web site owner's web page will appear as a "selectable" or "clickable" entry on your browser. You may then point your mouse to that web site selection, left click once and view that person's oranges web site.

The other common type of Internet search engine is called a "bot" - short for robot, or web-bot. This type of search seeks specific words directly from a web site's index page (the main or first page that appears when viewing a specific web site). If the word "oranges" appears on the first page of the web site, using the example above, the search robot will find it and return that web site's address as a selectable entry. Search engines usually return many web pages for you to select.

As with most obsessive-compulsive disorders, Internet browsing needs to be practiced to become proficient at it. As your addiction to the Internet grows, you will most likely find yourself arguing with the kids about who gets the computer and for how long. Your spouse will leave you when you spend 24 consecutive hours on the Internet, your pupils become fixed and dilated and you wear Depends while sitting at the computer. For those already addicted, there is a wonderful web site that offers help for your disorder; you can find it on the Internet at www.there-is-no-cure.com. (This is a joke. There is no such web address. Please don't spend all day trying to find it! There are, however, many sites that both identify symptoms of Internet addiction and feeds your need to be "connected") (As a matter of fact, there is nothing in this paragraph which is remotely serious, except the part where I recommend that you practice browsing to get good at it).

Now what? Of course, the question arises about what to do when you decide to go full-timing in your RV. Several things need to be considered at this point. Will a regular sized computer fit into your RV or, for that matter, your new lifestyle? Serious consideration should be given to purchasing a laptop computer, but there is one caution about which you should be advised: If you intend to spend any amount of time in front of the computer, please consider this: All the things we have learned about ergonomics - the positions in which we hold our bodies to perform certain tasks - do not apply to laptops. If the keyboard is in just the right position, then the computer screen will not be anywhere near the correct viewing position. If you put the laptop on a dinette table, the screen might be in a good spot, but you may not be comfortable typing on the keyboard. My personal suggestion, to avoid a sore back, neck spasms and carpal tunnel syndrome, is to see if you can work a normal home style tower-type computer into the design of your motorhome. You WILL thank me for this advice.

Ensure that you mount the CPU (the box containing all the stuff that makes your machine work, including the CD-ROM, hard disk and floppy drives), in a sponge lined and well ventilated compartment. This will ensure that the unit will not tip over, be subjected to road shocks or overheat.

Finding a connection to an Internet Service Provider (ISP) on the road may be your biggest challenge. The difficulty here is that you would need to call a local phone number for your ISP. If your ISP is in Florida and you are in British Columbia, you may encounter a problem. There are a few nationwide ISP's which may have 800 or 888 numbers that you can connect to via telephone connections found at most campgrounds. The larger ISPs, such as AOL have local access phone numbers all over the country. The other option is to carry a cellular or digital phone, also for connection to a National ISP's 800 or 888 phone line. All necessary equipment for the connection of a cell phone to the Internet is available from your local cell phone company. Remember that if you wish to connect on the road by cell phone, you will be paying for cellular air time, any long distance toll charges (if no 800 or 888 service is available) and connection time to your ISP. This can be a costly option, but expenses can be reduced substantially by connecting to the Internet in non-peak times.

In conclusion, I would like to wish you a safe, healthy and memorable motorhoming experience, be it a short trip, a vacation or full-timing. If you choose to become one of over 100 million Internet users, take it on the road as a valuable resource for just about anything you may need to know - from local attractions, roadside help or just plain entertainment, to keeping in touch with the family, chatting with friends or keeping the rest of the connected world up to date with your travels.

Most of all - Enjoy :-)

Editor's Note:

Ian Giffin earned a Diploma in Computer Programming from Control Data Institute in Toronto, Ontario, Canada in 1972. Ian has been driving buses since 1976 for such notable companies as the Toronto Transit Commission; Laidlaw School Bus Service, where he was with the Safety and Training Division; Wheel-Trans Mobility Impaired Transit in Toronto where he was one of 3 drivers testing the prototype Orion II wheelchair access bus; and most recently, Have Bus Will Travel, a V.I.P charter coach operation based in Southern Ontario. A full-time professional firefighter, Ian is also the owner of Bus Nut Online, a web site devoted to the hobby of converting a parlor coach into a motorhome. His web site can be found on the Internet at www.busnut.com.

Electronics and Entertainment

The motor coaches of today have all the electronic toys we enjoy in our homes. Twenty years ago, the best television reception we could expect was obtained with bat wing antennas. These were often marginal in fringe areas. It is common today to have the small eighteen inch satellite receiver dish mounted on the coach roof. Furthermore, many of these units are automatic in that they will elevate, seek and fine turn themselves only by the touch of a button.

A complete television system in a modern motor coach will consist of several elements. A cable attach point will permit cable reception offered by many RV parks. A selector, or splitter will send this signal to one or several television sets. Many coaches will have a video tape player to enjoy when it is inconvenient to either connect to cable or receive an ether-borne signal. Other choices will be a video tape recorder, whereby a program may be taped for later viewing. Some systems may include a video game system to keep the kids busy. Finally, the antenna may be of the satellite receiver dish or a simple bat-wing antenna with a booster.

If a satellite receiver is chosen, it might be convenient to include a dual LNB signal feed horn. The feed horn is the device at the end of the arm located at the focal point of the parabolic dish. This will permit two sets to operate simultaneously showing two separate programs. Of course, each set requires it's own satellite down load converter. This is why a dual LNB is needed.

Most television sets today have the capability of accepting at least two, or more, signals, which may be switched by the viewer. In addition, TVs also provide *surround sound*; the capability of sending sound to another set of speakers to be placed behind the viewer. This way the viewer is surrounded by the sound.

Stereo equipment is common in motor coaches today. This will consist of AM-FM receivers, dual tape decks and CD changers. These stereo systems may be united with the television systems in order to conserve speakers. That is, the stereo equipment may also use the same speaker system in use by the television systems.

Comfort and Convenience Producing Things

Things in our motor coaches which produce comfort are heaters, both air and water, and air conditioners. Those which produce convenience are such things as toilets, stoves, refrigerators. As a writer, I have been avoiding this chapter since it is bound to be dull but necessary. After all, how exciting can a furnace be? Unless, that is, it starts a major fire, or it won't even light off in sub zero temperature.

Many of our appliances, (and that is

what this chapter is all about) are a scaled down version of our home appliances designed to run on propane or minimal power and able to be tucked away in small places. So, lets list them and I will take them up, one at a time.

1. Comfort Heaters
   - Propane fired forced air
   - Propane fired boiler with circulating pump and radiant fins
   - Diesel fired boiler with circulating pump and air blower heat exchanger
   - Electric heaters
   - Wood burning fireplaces ???
2. Air Conditioners
   - Roof mounted units
   - Split air coolers
   - Evaporative coolers
   - Vents
   - Power vents
3. Cooking appliances
   - Propane fired combination range/oven
   - Microwave oven
   - Electric cook top
   - Toaster
   - Wok

Barbecue

4. Food Storage
   - Propane fired refrigerator
   - Electric Refrigerator
   - Pantry
   - Freezers

5. Toilet
   - Plastic
   - Porcelain
   - Power toilet

6. Water Heater
   - Propane fired
   - Electric
   - Radiator heat exchanger
   - Solar

As you can surmise, this chapter is designed for reference and may become quite dull before it is over. Many of the items discussed are my opinion and are not necessarily an authoritative maintenance manual. That sort of thing is available from the manufacturer.

Comfort Heaters

In most motorhomes and lower cost conversions, propane is the fuel of choice. Propane is an odorless gas, and is one of the fractions of crude oil. An agent is added to propane which gives it a distinctive odor of strong garlic. A propane leak is very easy to detect with its distinctive smell.

The RV industry has developed many options for propane heaters. The most common propane heater is the forced air type, which takes in outside air to support combustion, exhausts the products of combustion to the outside, and heats a radiator section over which air is blown. This heated air may be blown directly into the living compartment, or directed through a series of 4-inch ducts to strategic locations. The outlet of these ducts may be controlled with a register which may be throttled with dampers, or movable vanes used to attenuate the flow of air. The most significant drawback to this type of heater is its poor efficiency rating. Since, for safety, it must draw in outside air for combustion and expel these products of combustion, much of the heat is pumped overboard. This is patently obvious if you have ever stood next to one of these exhaust ports in the winter and felt the heat being expelled. Regardless of this inefficiency, propane as a heating fuel is relatively inexpensive, and these heaters can do an effective job of heating a coach. Such units are normally installed in a closet, or inside a table, or beneath a bench seat, or even in the baggage compartment, so one side is adjacent to an outside wall. Most are thermostatically controlled and are operated by a 12VDC current.

Several brands names are available for this type of furnace. They are: Suburban, by Dometic, and Hydra-Flame, by Hydra-Flame.

Diesel Boiler

The heart of the diesel boiler system is a package about the size of two footballs, end to end. It uses engine radiator coolant pumped past a diesel burner, then circulated throughout the coach to individual radiators, or radiant finned units with individual fans similar to baseboard heaters, to extract the heat and deliver it to each compartment. The coolant is then recirculated to the burner section to repeat the action. One system uses a single loop, so by the time it is nearing the end of its loop, most of the heat has already been extracted. A more efficient system uses two loops. One loop circulates only hot water while the other loop returns cooler water whose heat has been extracted. Makeup water to the burner is drawn from a reservoir, while the return cool water is delivered to the reservoir. This system is thermostatically controlled, which automatically ignites the burner, activates the circulating pump, and turns on the fans at the individual radiator units. One major advantage to this system is it also serves as an engine preheater, since engine coolant may be circulated through a heat exchanger. This can be a very useful thing in cold weather. Diesel engines can be very stubborn to start when cold.

Several brands of this type of heating system are available. Probably the most well known brand of this type heating system is the Webasto. The Webasto system comprises the boiler heating a coolant in a closed loop, supplying heat to various fan/heater elements back through an expansion tank to be recirculated. Although copper piping with its soldered joints is an ideal material for circulating the coolant, the risk of fire from the installation and soldering of the pipe and its fittings has caused other materials to be used. An excellent substitute for the copper piping is ¾-inch diameter heater hose. The hose may be swept in gradual turns, and where an abrupt bend is needed, a copper fitting prepared outside the coach may be coupled with the hose. The spring loaded type hose clamps are recommended since they apply a constant pressure regardless of the temperature. There are also various high temperature plastic piping systems now available which will function in a satisfactory manner. The maximum temperature routed through the heating system is 180 degrees Fahrenheit.

The coolant for the heating system must be a mixture of 50/50 — water and antifreeze. This circuit will be totally independent from the coach engine cooling, but through a heat exchanger may be used to preheat the motor. The circuit is normally a parallel circuit sending hot water out to the various fan/heater units and returning cooler water to the boiler through and expansion tank. It is essential the expansion tank be above the level of the boiler, and accessible. This tank is often placed inside a closet. In this circuit it is mandatory there be no air entrapment. In the event small bubbles are encountered, the boiler may cause a high temperature safety fuse to burn out and the unit will not function until it has been replaced. It is for this reason, the water circuit be isolated from the engine coolant, in that tiny bubbles can develop in the engine water that are eventually eliminated through the radiator cap. The flow rate of the coolant is normally about 6 gallons per minute so that ¾-inch hose provides adequate flow rate over about 100 feet of circuitry and three full flow fan/heater units.

Heat exchangers are available for not only preheating the engine, but for providing domestic hot water for bathing and cooking. In addition, electric water heaters are available with built in heat exchangers so hot water may be obtained from shore power, generator power, or from the Webasto boiler unit. Circuitry has been developed so in summer months when no heat is needed, the boiler will supply hot water to the heat exchanger for domestic hot water.

Diesel fuel to the boiler unit should

have its own supply line rather than teeing-off of the main fuel line to the engine. A tee intersecting the main engine supply fuel line has been tried in the past and has consistently caused problems. The fuel supply to the boiler unit is similar to the engine in that it has a supply and a return. A specific tank should be dedicated to the heating unit for reasons mentioned earlier in this book; the lesser cost off-road fuel may be used for heating. This tank should supply both the heating system and the generator.

The generator should be mounted in such a manner it may be accessible for maintenance and it would be a good idea to provide soundproofing around the containment box. Both the boiler and the circulating pump can be noisy. A further contributor to the high noise level is the exhaust pipe, which must be routed outside.

Individual fan/heaters are available to be placed in strategic locations. These units, on average, produce about 7,000 BTUs each. The entire system may be controlled by thermostats, or a combination of thermostats. For example, three units may be controlled by a thermostat in the living room/kitchen area, and another two units may be controlled by a thermostat in the bathroom, or bedroom area. Another more passive heater is available in the form of a baseboard finned unit. The baseboard finned units can be had in the form of 2 x 2 inch fins along a ¾-inch pipe in almost any length. These non fan baseboard heaters are customarily set about 1½ inches above the floor or carpet along the baseboard. The cold dense air slides down the wall from the windows, is heated by convection and rises to replace the cold air. Another fan/heater unit from Webasto is the toe-kick size which may be installed under the cabinet in the recessed kick area such as a bathroom cabinet or the kitchen counter. Each of the fan/heater units have either an in-line or elbow air bleed fitting on the downstream side to make sure no air resides in the circuitry.

The Webasto coolant heaters can be ordered in 12VDC and 24VDC configurations and have heating capacities ranging from 16,000 Btus to 160,000 BTUs. Perhaps the most useful size for a conversion is the Model DWB2010 whose output is 40,000 BTUs. Webasto also markets an air heater with capacities ranging from 6,000 BTUs to 40,000 BTUs. I am currently unaware of any converted coach employing the use of the Webasto air heaters. The average electrical power consumption is about 5½ amperes at 12VDC, and about a gallon of diesel fuel per hour.

A competitor to the Webasto is a newer product with the trade name ProHeat, manufactured by Teleflex. This unit was originally developed as an engine pre-heater for large diesel trucks operating in very cold areas of North America. ProHeat produces two sizes, a 30,000 Btu and a 50,000 Btu unit. Since the ProHeat device is a much newer product than the Webasto, it employs newer technology. It has a computerized controller with memory which may be down loaded into a personal computer. This allows the system to be diagnosed by a service station to determine the last 50 starts, to see if, for example, a low voltage was present. Other readouts include number of hours, water temperature, number of cycles and other parameters. It also uses a compressor to finely atomize the combustion air to the fuel nozzle for more efficient burning.

The big market for the ProHeat is the trucking industry, not converted coach sales. Hence, service stations are being located all over the country. These units are being installed on new trucks for several reasons. The newer engines such as the Detroit Series 60 do not produce sufficient heat for heating the cab, so auxiliary heaters must be employed. In addition, due to the Clean Air Act, in many location trucks are not permitted to idle. So again, auxiliary heaters must be used. Many of the newer production coaches are including diesel fired boilers for passenger heat and defrosting.

The ProHeat system is comparable to the Webasto in performance and cost. The principal difference is the ProHeat is a newer design using the latest technology. And because of the truck market, more service stations are available. An approximate cost for a complete ProHeat system, is about $3,300. This figure includes four space heaters, thermostats, valves, expansion tank, a heat exchanger for engine heat, and a heat exchanger domestic water heater. Again, this represents the components, less the piping and installation labor.

The AquaHot system uses the Webasto heater, but is effectively an engineered system with all controls and plumbing, and is probably the top of the line when it comes to diesel heating for motor coaches.

Propane Fired Boiler

The Primus system, the principle propane boiler, is similar to the Webasto except for the fuel. The Primus system has similar types of heaters as Webasto, but they stress the passive radiant fin baseboard type. It may be considered the top of the line for propane. It yields a pleasant and clean heat, eliminating dust, drafts and condensation problems. It is virtually soundless without fans or blowers. As such, it doesn't blow dust around the coach and is considered healthy. It provides a uniformly, consistent heat with normally only about a 2 degree temperature difference from the floor to the ceiling.

The combustion unit is located outside the living area so there is no worry about carbon monoxide poisoning. Only hot water enters the living quarters and electronic ignition eliminates the danger of a pilot light. Since the heat transfer medium is a mixture of 50/50 water/automotive antifreeze, there is no problem in winterizing the system.

Electric Heaters

Electric heating generally costs more than energy obtained from the combustion of a fuel, but the convenience, cleanliness, and reduced space needs of electric heat can often justify its use. The heat can be provided from electric coils or strips used in varying patterns. For example, convectors may be in or on the walls, under windows, or as baseboard radiation. Electric heating is one of the safer forms of heat. In addition to being safe, the electric heater also is convenient to install, and might be located in areas which are unused. Since heated air tends to be displaced by colder more dense air, consequently rising, the obvious location for a heater, regardless of their energy source, is near the floor.

One form of an electric heater is a small thermostatically controlled unit mounted in the toe-kick area underneath cabinets and furniture. The unit is appropriately call the Perfect-Toe. This unit is 3½ inches high, and 17 inches wide, by 10 inches deep. It is capable of producing 1000 watts of heat, and has a built-in thermostat switch. To compare this output with our heat load in BTUs, each kilowatt-hour of electricity equals 3412 BTUs. Each one of these toe-kick heaters generate 3412 BTUs. The only drawback to this unit is that each unit has its own controls, so that they are not centrally controlled. However, a simple circuit could be designed that would control all the units in a coach from a single thermostat, after each unit had been tuned to its optimum performance.

Another form of electric heat is the baseboard heater. One drawback to this design is that much of the baseboard inside a coach is occupied by built-in furniture, or other permanently mounted facilities.

Wood Burning Fireplaces

This is supposed to be a joke, but I have a friend who actually mounted a small fireplace inside his coach. I have seen some old *hippie* coaches with pot bellied stoves for heat. Obviously, the danger they present is the consumption of all the oxygen in the compartment and production of deadly carbon monoxide and the hazard of fire.

Catalytic Heaters

Another, more effective form of propane heater, is the catalytic heater. This heater uses a platinum mesh and fiber matrix which allows the fuel to burn without a flame. The burning in this matrix will glow and produces a radiant form of heat. It is actually a form of convection combined with radiation, with the prominent form being radiation. These units are mounted as a wall unit, which is a draw back since wall space in a conversion is at a premium.. The less sophisticated units use a mechanical pizzo-electric igniter, similar to those seen on barbecues. While striking the igniter, a gas valve must be held down to light the pilot. After the pilot is lit, the main gas valve may be opened as desired. This unit requires no electric power to the installation, only a source of propane. The Olympia catalytic heater is an example of this kind.

The Platinum Cat, produced by Thermal Systems of Washington, is a well engineered catalytic heater which uses a tiny blower to vent products of combustion through a small duct to the outside, and is thermostatically controlled with an auto matic igniter. The unit must be supplied with a 12VDC power source, along with a supply of propane. Again, the unit must be mounted on a vertical surface similar to the old fashioned wall heaters installed in the cheapest houses built after World War II. I have seen this unit installed in an area over the driver's section located behind cabinet doors. This form of installation is not recommended, but with adequate heat shields on the inside of the cabinets, and doors, and with a fail-safe interlock so the unit is disabled when the doors are closed, this installation appears to be satisfactory.

Heat Pumps

For background purposes a brief discussion of heat pumps is included. A heat pump is a system designed to provide useful heating and cooling, and its actions are essentially the same for either process. Instead of creating heat, as does a furnace, the heat pump transfers heat from one place to another. In cold weather, a liquid refrigerant such as Freon, is pumped through a coil which is outside the area to be heated. The refrigerant is cold, so it absorbs heat from the outside air, the ground, well water, or some other source. It then flows first to a compressor, which raises its temperature and pressure so it becomes vapor before it flows to an indoor coil. There the warmth is radiated or blown into the room or other space to be heated. The refrigerant, having given up much of its heat, then flows through a valve where its pressure and temperature are lowered further, before it liquefies and is pumped into the outdoor coil to continue the cycle.

To air condition a space, valves reverse the flow so the refrigerant picks up heat from inside and discharges it outside. Like furnaces, most heat pumps are controlled by thermostats. Most heat pumps use atmospheric air as their heat source. This presents a problem in areas where winter temperatures frequently drop below freezing, making it difficult to raise the temperature and pressure of the refrigerant. Heat-pump systems are now being used extensively not only in residences but also in commercial buildings and schools.

Air Conditioning

Coleman manufactures a central air conditioning system which mounts out of sight, either on or under the floor of the coach. It is controlled by a wall thermostat and uses a system of ducts. The 2-Ton PLUS is basically two units in a single package. With moderate temperatures only one compressor is used, but when the temperature goes up, a second compressor kicks in.

Coleman claims with only one compressor in use, the system provides 20 percent more cooling than a comparable roof top unit, and 16 percent more with both compressors on compared with two rooftop units. They claim an airflow of twice that comparable to rooftop units. A significant advantage is a self-contained system without the need for pre-charged lines which may leak coolant. It may be located at any convenient place in the coach as long as it is adjacent to an outside wall, so as to permit the heat gathered in the condenser to exhaust to the outside. The condenser opening is approximately 15 x 33 inches. Properly designed duct work is essential for effective operation. Ducts should be sized per the manual and located as recommended. The unit occupies a space of 16½ x 21 x 44 inches.

Split Air Conditioning Systems

Split units are so named because they separate the compressor and condenser from the evaporator and fan as two separate units. This is similar to residential systems in which the compressor and condenser are normally placed outside the house, while the evaporator and blower reside inside the building. In a similar fashion, the split units are separated, so the fan and evaporator may be installed in an overhead cabinet with its small blower or fan. The compressor and condenser are then placed in the baggage compartment and are ventilated in such a manner the heat extracted from the condenser is dumped overboard or outside the coach. It is important the exhaust air passing through the condenser is removed from the compartment in a way that it cannot be re-ingested by the blower delivering air to the condenser. If this condition exists, the refrigeration process will be severely limited, since the whole process is one of extracting heat from the living area and exhausting it to the outside. This is one of the reason air conditioning systems tend to loose their effectiveness as the outside temperature increases.

Another physical process occurring during the refrigeration cycle is the condensation of ambient air in the living quarters. This condensation occurs when the inside air passes over the cooling coils, (the evaporator). The moisture contained in the inside air contains a normal saturation point at the existing temperature. As it passes over the chilled coils, the saturated air drops below its dew point (condensation temperature). This causes the moisture in the air to liquefy, on the cooling coils creating condensation. A collection pan is normally designed into the evaporator section with a stub tube so a drain tube may be attached and allow the condensation water to drain overboard.

Several split units are customarily placed at strategic locations throughout the coach. Normally these units are available in ratings of 8,000 to 12,000 BTU, so they may be designed to create a selective cooling system, i.e., they may be located in such a manner to employ your electrical power to the most advantageous usage. Again, it is important to stress the effectiveness of a refrigerated cooling system is its ability to dispel the heat extracted from the cooled space.

Split units are made so they are pre-charged with refrigerant at the factory. They are connected with pre-charged lines. These lines are soft copper for flexibility, and have end fittings so they can be connected at each end. The ends are pierced to allow the coolant to move between each component. In addition, the lower component (the condenser/compressor unit) has Schroeder type valves (similar to the inflation valves on tires), so at any time the system needs charging it may be done by an independent refrigeration technician.

Split units are not uncommon and were originally developed for the mobile home industry. Many mobile home and RV supply companies market these systems

Roof Air Conditioning Units

Roof air conditioning units are the most common in the R.V. industry. For one thing, they are relatively inexpensive, and are self contained. They easily and effectively get rid of the condenser heat, and are quite satisfactory in performance. In addition, they are easy to install, and in a worst case scenario, they are simply replaced. Roof-airs are installed over a standard 14-inch square opening. Roof air conditioners are now being made in units up to 15,000 Btus, so two or three units should cool a conversion adequately.

The roof A/C unit may also be remotely controlled with a thermostat. The Coleman company makes available a remote control unit which may be connected to their standard roof units. This allows the use of a ceiling fixture, which may be combined with lighting designed to conceal the normal roof A/C interior unit. Some quite dazzling ceiling fixtures have been installed in some bus conversions.

The most disagreeable feature of the roof air conditioning unit is the sound level of the blower delivering cooled air to the interior. For those of you sensitive to excessive noise levels, other solutions should be sought. Not only does the blower create a lot of noise, but the compressor, even the rotary type, contributes to the unpleasant noise factor.

Another drawback to the roof air conditioning unit, is the external appearance. Some liken its appearance to a window air conditioning unit, but instead of sticking out of a window, it is sticking out of the roof. In some coaches, this may also be hazardous by causing an over-height condition. When you consider that the average floor height of a bus conversion is nearly five feet from the ground, then add another seven feet of interior height and structure, we are very close to 12 feet of height without any roof protuberances. If roof air conditioning units are employed, it is a wise practice to know your overall height and check the clearance of every underpass you come to. This is especially true back east where many older underpasses only had to allow clearance for a hay wagon.

I recall one time I was lost in New Bedford, Mass., and a courteous gentleman offered to lead me out of town. The first underpass he went through had a ten foot clearance, so I continued another block and found an underpass with a 13'-6" clearance. Fortunately, my guide came back and led me out of town to I-95. Our personal coach has an overall height of 12'-6".

We have the roof airs extending nine inches above the roof. The new 15,000 Btu units are 12 inches in height

Other Options

Another form of air conditioning which should be mentioned is the least expensive type, the common window air conditioner. Although this type of unit is not recommended for coach conversions, I have seen some clever modifications and installations of this system. The principal problem is that the window A/C is designed to eliminate condenser heat through natural convection into the outside air, and with a conversion, we don't have the luxury of protuberances sticking out of our normal contour. In addition to spoiling the beauty of the coach, it increases our aerodynamic drag and exceeds the allowable width limit by law. The installations I have seen create a large plenum inside the coach to exhaust the heat, and bring the makeup air from another source, such as a wheel well. This permits the complete unit to remain inside of the original coach contour. Again, I would discourage anyone from using this type of cooler, since it requires considerable innovation, occupies more space than necessary, and may, or may not work.

Heat Pumps

Although Cruisair could fit into the split air category, it is the only system I am currently aware of which can also be ordered as a heat pump. Hence, it is presented in the heat pump category.

The Cruisair total comfort system gives you great flexibility in directing airflow throughout the coach. A single condensing unit can support more than one cooling/heating unit, and air can be ducted from a single cooling/heating unit to two separate areas. Cruisair's Applications Engineering Department renders assistance in laying out and specifying the best system for a given coach. Cruisair systems are available for cooling only or for heating and cooling.

The combined cooling/heating system works just like a home-type heat pump. The system contains a reversing valve which permits the condensing unit to function as a heat pump extracting ambient heat from the outside air. The reversing valve is controlled by the cabin switch assembly and provides for automatic change-over between the cooling and heating modes to maintain the thermostat set point. The Cruisair heat pump provides heating efficiency at outside temperatures down to 40 degrees F. For regular use in very cold temperatures, auxiliary duct heat-modules can be installed to provide warm airflow using the same ducts and grills as the air conditioning system. A variety of auxiliary heating options are available, and Cruisair Applications Engineers can help you choose. Condensing units are available in 14,000 BTU/hr models. The units are hermetically sealed for safe operation. Ventilation is required for the air-cooled refrigerant condenser, but the unit is not affected by moisture or vibration. Condensing units use fans or squirrel-cage blowers to move air across the coil. Blower models normally take air in through the coil in front and discharge it through the bottom of the unit. Fan-type units take air in the back and discharge it through the coil in front.

All Cruisair motor coach air conditioning systems are designed for 115V single-phase 60 Hz power, but 230V systems can be built on special order.

Appliances

I won't waste a lot of ink on such mundane items as cook tops and ovens, except to point out those features of RV appliances which are different from normal household appliances. Propane ranges use a pilot light similar to old fashioned residential ranges. It is necessary to light off this pilot each time you inhabit your coach. The more modern ranges use an electronic ignition similar to modern water heaters.

The electric cooktop is often installed in the very expensive motor coaches and bus conversions because the coaches are all electric. Microwave ovens are always electric, except for an ad I once saw promoting a kerosene fired microwave oven for camping use. Do you believe that? If you can find one, let me know about it.

Refrigerator

Probably the most mysterious appliance in a motor coach for a novice is the propane fired refrigerator. It does not perform anything like the "ice box" at home. Instead of an electric energy gobbling compressor, the RV box uses the absorption cooling system. This uses a propane burner to boil an ammonia mixture, which evaporates chilling the freezer section. The mixture then recondenses and repeats the cycle. This process is exceptionally energy efficient

Since the absorption refrigeration cycle is such that it exhausts the heat extracted to the ambient conditions, the hotter the outside weather, the poorer performance you will see. There are a number of steps one can take to insure maximum performance. If your coach has been parked for a while with the "frig" off, light it off a day before you begin a trip. This allows it to *chill out* and stabilize before you add your contents. The items you are planning to keep refrigerated should already be chilled in your household refrigerator. This will permit your RV unit to loaf.

Don't let frost build up. Frost insulates the chilling fins and reduces the performance of your unit. To minimize frost, wipe any moisture off before storing anything. Keep container lids tight so moisture can't escape to form frost. Arrange your food so adequate air might circulate. Don't allow anything on the shelves to block the flow of air. In really warm weather, it is a good idea to place one of those small battery operated fans inside to help circulate the air.

When removing or placing food in the unit, do so as quickly as practical. Long open door exposure reduces the efficiency as it would any refrigerator. Be sure the door gasket seals properly. Be sure the flue and ventilation door are completely free. A blocked flue on the roof, or a restricted ventilation door, will reduce the performance drastically.

One of the problems while traveling, is keeping the burner lit. A severe cross wind can extinguish the burner and you are driving along fat, dumb, and happy and when you reach for a cold beer at the end of a long day, it ain't cold! And, the potato salad is spoiled and the lettuce has wilted and the *frig* doesn't smell too good. We have found a pretty good answer to this problem by installing a standard furnace air filter just behind the ventilation door. This filter buffers the wind gusts responsible for blowing out the fire but allows enough oxygen to support combustion.

The newer three-way units which have been available for about ten years, will operate on propane, 12 volt DC and 120 volt AC. They seek the most appropriate power source and automatically switch to it. It is my personal opinion a refrigerator should never have the option of working on 12 volts DC. The theory is while cruising down the road the coach alternator supplies the necessary 12 volts to support the "frig." The theory may be OK but I have seen batteries depleted by this process..

Power management for our refrigerator is to keep it plugged in while at home in the barn. But while on the road, en route, we keep the unit switched to gas. This is true even when we are temporarily plugged in at a park over night. It is too easy to forget to switch back to gas if we switch to electric for an overnight stay. Some will argue it is a waste of propane not to switch to electric when possible but our experience has been our propane use for water heating, cooking , heating and refrigerator power, averages about a quart a day. In today's market that translates to 25 cents a day.

If you have to park your rig in a storage lot remote from home, clean out the refrigerator and turn it off. Leave the door cracked to allow air to circulate, otherwise, you will probably have a nice crop of mold.

Years ago, there was a product made for motor coach refrigerators known as a Frig Lock. The gadget was a rather gross looking device designed to insure your frig stayed closed while in transit. From time to time it tended to get a little out of adjustment and fail to do its job and occasionally the frig door would swing open and a carton of milk would slosh all over the floor. Today the modern frig uses a pretty reliable latch and the milk bath hasn't happened recently.

The high end, all electric bus conversions will probably have a standard residential refrigerator. These require 120 volt AC power at all times. Their power consumption will vary but when in daily use, will use about 50 amps per day. This is only about 6KW but is not supportable by a normal battery bank without a large generator and invertor.

Toilets

There are three major suppliers of toilets for motor coaches: Thetford, Sealand, and Microphor. Each one is different from the other. The Thetford unit is a plastic body and dumps straight down through a valve as does the Sealand. The Sealand has a porcelain body, however. The Microphor toilet is the Cadillac of the RV toilets in that it is porcelain and uses a vacuum system similar to that used on large sea going ships. As can be expected the prices vary according to the level of performance.

One comment I have, is the Sealand comes in two seat heights. For older guys, (of which I am) the higher unit is more convenient. Further, if you have a low toilet height, consider building the base up so you won't have so far to squat.

Water Heaters

There are few things as delightful as hot water, especially when in the shower. And, not many things equal the disappointment of cold water when stepping into a shower. Water heaters for motor coaches are varied and many. There are six gallon tanks, ten gallon tanks, electric fired, propane fired and heat exchanger fired.

Most of us have at least a 50 gallon water heater in our homes, so the question is often asked, " How can a six gallon water heater satisfy our needs?" The answer is, six gallons of hot water mixed with six gallons of cold water, produce 12 gallons of warm comfortable shower water. Now, I know many of us luxuriate for a long time in the hot water of our shower at home, but in a motor coach we do not have the unlimited quantity of water supplied to our homes. We can, however, enjoy a normal cleansing and delightful shower in our coaches with less than five gallons of water.

I remember the days of the early RV water heaters which had to bc lit off by going outside and holding a match to a pilot as we held down the safety shut-off. Today, almost all propane water heaters use electronic ignition where the task of lighting the hot water heater is as difficult as pressing a switch. Furthermore, today's units are exceptionally efficient, requiring not much more than 15 minutes to reach temperature.

At one time, it was common to buy a three-way water heater; one which would use propane, electricity or engine radiator water for heating. The heat exchanger methods has been discouraged due the potential of corrosion causing a mixture of engine coolant into the potable water supply. Engine coolant contains glycol, which is a poisonous form of alcohol. My personal choice, is a six gallon propane fired water heater with a 120 volt electric heating element. This way, when we are on the road, the propane does the job, but when we are plugged into a park or at a wired friends place we switch to electric. Unlike the problem of forgetting to switch back to propane for our refrigerator, a little cold water will heat up quickly enough so as not to be a problem.

Gauges and Monitors

Lon Cross

There are gauges for any type of system that you could want to install on your motorhome. Also, there are fewer gauges in a lower priced motorhome than in ones that are more expensive. Example, the number of gauges in an entry level, 23 foot, gas engine, class "C" is very sparse. Compare that class "C" to a 42 foot, diesel pusher, bus conversion whose instrument panel and console rival that of a Boeing 747. There also seems to be a trend throughout the RV industry where some gauges are being replaced by warning (idiot) lights. This reduces cost by not having to install expense measuring devices. The reason some motorhomes have more gauges than others is mainly due to the type of engines used. A diesel engine requires monitoring of more functions than that of a gas engine. The law of course does require certain gauges must be installed on all motor vehicles, e.g., speedometer, odometer, etc. Gauges can be broken into groups they monitor, i.e., engine, house and convenience.

Gauges usually come in two standard sizes, 2 inch and 3 inch diameters. However, the speedometer, odometer and tach are the most frequently observed and, therefore, should be a larger diameter that can be easily read. Gauges can either be analog or digital. The analog gauge is an electrical-mechanical device, usually housed in a round case, with a needle that points to the indicated number. Digital gauges are solid state devices that come in many sizes, and display their data in numerical digits. The two largest companies in the gauge business are Stewart-Warner and VDO.

Engine Gauges

Oil Pressure Gauge

All our lives we have heard of the importance of the engine oil pressure reading. Obviously, if there was no oil pressure, it would imply there was no oil, hence the motor would grind itself into a catastrophic failure. Another bit of information is available from this gauge. Diesel engines, especially the two-stroke Detroit, have a tendency to consume some of the lubricating oil in the reservoir. Because of this, the motor must have oil added periodically. As the oil level goes down, the oil pressure shown on the gauge will also go down, so this is the first indicator to check our reservoir with our dip stick. There are many options for pressure ranges so be sure to select a gauge appropriate for a diesel engine. This is normally zero to 80 pounds per square inch (psi). High RPM engines normally use gauges reading up to 100 psi. The Complete oil pressure indication system consists of a gauge, a transducer (sender), connecting wire, a DC source and a ground.

Water Temperature Gauge

Most of us have V8 motors in our rigs. Some of the older coaches use the in-line engine but for all practical purposes, our V8's are equivalent to two in-line 4 cylinder motors. Certainly these two halves drive the same crank shaft but it is important to be able to monitor each half separately. For this reason, we employ two water temperature gauges. It is entirely possible to have a problem on one side of the engine, with the other side functioning quite well. In fact, it is not uncommon to tear down and rebuild only one side of a V8 diesel engine.

The sources for a temperature sender, are many on a diesel motor. The temperature senders are easy to spot and are quite obvious. Just look around the area of the thermostat housings which are located at the ends of the cylinder heads. The senders are just a small screw-in fitting with an electrical terminal at the end.

Again, all that is required is a dial indicator (the gauge), a thermocouple (the sender), a connecting wire, a DC source, and a ground.

With our modern engines, and engine

coolant, with a tight pressure radiator system, we can safely operate up to 220 degrees Fahrenheit. But, keep in mind, most of us are driving older rigs and the ideal operating temperature of a two-stroke diesel is 180° F. and our coolant system may be a little tired. So, as a word to the wise, keep it below 200° F.

A very useful piece of insurance is a water spray system. This is nothing more than a PVC pipe supplied by the fresh water tank through a 12 volt solenoid valve controlled at the driver's position with a few hot house misters. This water spray will direct a fog onto the radiator and cool your motor in just a few minutes. Being mildly paranoid about a high temperature condition of my motor, I always turn on my water spray when the gauge reads 190°F. My paranoia stems from my earlier engine frying experience. Not a thing I am proud of.

Speedometer/Odometer

Have you ever noticed that while you have been traveling in a caravan, or convoy, as the *naivey boys* say, that you hear someone over their C.B. ask someone else what their speedometer is indicating. So, since we are all on the same frequency, we all hear the answer. And, pretty soon, every guy in the caravan is putting in his two cents. Doncha wonder why nobody agrees with each other. After all, we are all in sight of each other and the road is flat and level and there is no wind, so we should all be reading the same speed. This seems to be a chronic ailment of many motor coaches. Each of us, of course, are convinced that our instrument is precise, but some of us know better, but won't admit it.

Actual speed is subject to engine speed, transmission ratios, rear end ratios, and tire size. So, all kinds of little gears are assembled at speedometer shops to get the indicator right. Some speedometers have to be tweaked while driving a measured mile course. We do have one gage, however, that isn't subject to all these variables, our tachometer. If we assume that our tachometer is accurate, and an electric tach is usually pretty close (less than one percent error), we may then write a formula to compute our actual speed, by taking into account the variables listed above.

For simplicity, lets assume that our

transmission is in one to one ratio., that is, we are in high gear (no overdrive), with our drive shaft turning at the same RPM as our engine. If we wish to determine another ratio, we divide our results by the increased ratio. We then multiply the tire diameter in inches times Pi, (3.14159), and multiply that by our RPM and again multiply that by 60, and divide this by our rearend ratio, which will gives us the number of inches we travel in one hour. We then divide that number by 12 and again by 5280, and finally we have it! Our speed in miles per hour.

The above logic gives us the following formula:

$$MPH = \frac{60 \times d \times Pi \times RPM}{12 \times 5280 \times R}$$

$$MPH = \frac{d \times PI \times RPM}{1056 \times R}$$

where: d = tire diameter
Pi = Pi (3.14159)
RPM = Tachometer reading
R = Rearend Ratio

Most of our forty foot highway coaches have a rear-end ratio of 3.71, and many of us are using 11R22.5 tires with a diameter of 42 inches. So, simplifying the above equation we get:

MPH = .03377 times RPM

Now this is pretty darned close to one third of ten percent of the rpm. So, if you are doing 1800 rpm, drop a zero, and divide by three, and voila, you get 60 miles per hour. If you have 11R24.5 tires add five percent and you get 63 miles per hour.

So, now that we have that problem solved to everyone's satisfaction, it's now time to ask your caravanning buddies what they are turning, i.e., tachometer reading. Just see how many coaches agree with each other.

The purpose of the speedometer needs no explanation. However, unlike hot rods and roadsters, we do not need to have a speed range over 80 mph. With the standard rear-end, and wheel diameters, our rigs are just about maxed-out at 78 miles per hour. This figure corresponds to and defines a speed of 2250 rpm, a 3.71 rear end ratio and

11R24.5 tires.

The odometer is a meter which records mileage. So, this gauge is useful to determine trip length, distance between points and our fuel economy. Many of the modern units also have a re-settable trip meter which is again, useful for calculating miles per gallon. We simply reset the trip meter each time we refuel.

The speedometer and the tachometer are two gauges which are normally 3 inches in diameter.

Some speedometers are driven with a magnetic sensor mounted by a wheel. The electric speedometer, however, uses a small electric motor mounted at the transmission and adjusted with a series of gears. A speedometer shop will commonly install a gear combination and tape a counter along side of the bus. By driving a measured mile, known to the speedometer technician, the counter will register a number which allows him to assemble a combination of gears. The gear combination will be installed at your transmission and connected to the sender. An accurate speed indication and mileage, will then result on your gauge in the cockpit.

Another form of speedometer has an

adjustment screw in the back. This requires that someone drive the bus at a constant indicated speed and the distance recorded according to mile markers along side of the road per the time. Adjustment can then be made until an accurate speed is indicated. Stewart - Warner and VDO employ the motor-generator style sender which must be adjusted with gear combinations.

Tachometers

The tachometer sender is unique in that it is normally coupled to the cam shaft drive in the Detroit engine used by buses. Sometimes the tach drive is on the bell housing side of the motor and other times it is on the front of the engine. A flange is normally in place with a cap similar to a pipe cap. This cap is removed and the sender is screwed in place with a drive tang. This tang engages a quill which is pressed into the end of the cam shaft. Some motors do not have this quill in place and it is necessary to purchase this drive quill from a Detroit dealer and install it. This quill has a multi-splined end which may be pressed or lightly tapped into the end of the cam shaft. The other end has a hole and slot which will accept the tach drive tang.

The tang is about an inch or so long with a square shape at one end (this goes into the tach sender motor) and a key shape on the other end which is inserted into the drive quill. There are many tang options so it is important to select the one which matches with your quill and your tach sender. The tach sender has a female threaded end which screwed on the engine boss. It is then, again, a simple matter to couple the gauge and the sender motor with wire.

Fuel Pressure Gauge

A fuel pressure gauge is an especially useful instrument for a diesel motor. One thing which will slow you down and diminish your performance is dirty fuel filters, both primary and secondary. When should you change these filters? In my early days I recall traveling in Wyoming on what seemed to be a nearly flat section of terrain. The coach gradually lost speed and regardless of my pressure on the throttle it continued to slow down. My wife, the astute one, suggested I change the fuel filter. Acknowledging her wisdom, I complied with her suggestion. Wow! The old rig took on new life. A little later it began to slow down again. She queried, "Did you change both the primary and the secondary filters?" Admitting I only changed the primary, I went to the back and replaced the secondary filter. After this, the "old gal" acted like a teenager again (the coach that is).

If you cannot find a gage marked fuel pressure, use an oil pressure gauge and sender. After all, all you are really interested in is the relative value of fuel pressure with new filters versus the value of the fuel pressure with dirty filters. With a 100 psi pressure gauge, the fuel pressure reading will indicate about 60 psi with clean filters and about 15 with dirty filters needing to be replaced.

A standard fuel pressure gauge will normally read 1 to 15 psi. In any event, what you are concerned with is not the absolute number but the relative number which indicates when you should replace your filters.

Fuel Gauges

I have yet to find many older coaches with an operable fuel gauge. The Silver Eagles bus, as an example, uses VDO instruments. Their fuel gauge sender is a float inside a vertically oriented tube about 22" long. With a new sender and a new gauge, an indication of fuel on board is reasonably accurate. With age, however, these senders often become stuck in one position, or the wiring comes loose or gets knocked off.

The Stewart-Warner fuel gage is not suitable in many cases, since it uses a "broken arm" type sender, similar to a toilet float valve . This float stays on top of the fuel changing the resistance of a rheostat at the hinge point with the instrument needle reflecting the changing voltage and calibrated in quantity, that is, empty, ¼, ½, ¾, and full. The reason this sender will not work is the internal baffling in the tank will interfere with the sender not allowing it to operate. This problem can be eliminated by having a custom tank fabricated.

Another approach to accurate fuel management is a dip stick similar to that used to check your oil. Again, you must compensate for the baffling and use a flexible dip stick. A piece of steel strapping material works well in this application. The stick or strap then only need be calibrated for gallons. Using the formula: (Width x Length x Height [in inches]) divided by 231 will give you the number of gallons in the tank. Fill the tank and mark the dip stick. Mark the stick in 5 gallon increments and you will always know how much fuel you have and you will be able to determine your fuel economy.

And then, there is the old fashioned sight gauge which is nothing more than a transparent tube connected to a pair of fittings at the top and bottom of the tank. This is probably the most accurate form of fuel gauge available.

Another form of liquid level gauge was brought out a few years back. It is simply a tube inserted into the tank with an open end near the bottom. As the tank is filled, a level of pressure is generated inside the tube as part of the liquid attempts to penetrate the tube causing a gauge to react to the increased pressure. In effect, the gauge is reading the difference between atmospheric and hydrostatic pressure. When the tank is empty, the gauge will read zero because all there is is atmospheric pressure; when the tank is full, the gage will read the hydrostatic pressure of the number of inches of the liquid type and read this figure as being full. All the gauge has to be calibrated for, is empty and full.

Transmission Temperature Gauge

The transmission temperature gauge is simply a monitor to assess the condition of your automatic transmission. The Allison 700 series is so over-designed for the weight and performance of our coach engines, it is a rare condition that would cause a problem.

For example, the 700 series are also installed in 80,000 pound semi-trucks and in earthmovers. So, although we consider our coaches to be beefy vehicles, they don't really compare to those just mentioned.

However, it is always a good idea to have an oil temperature gauge where one is possible. I have found from personal experience, it is wise to purchase an automatic transmission oil temperature gauge and sender recommended by the manufacturer.

For example, an Allison transmission should use a gauge with the name Allison on it. This gauge will be very general as to the specific temperature, but will display an operating zone of safety.

The gauge comes with a matched sender which is installed in an appropriate port in the body of the transmission. It is then a simple matter to wire the sender to the gauge

Turbocharger Vacuum Boost Gauge

The vacuum boost gage for your turbocharger, if your engine is so equipped, is normally designed to read in inches of mercury. 30 inches of mercury is pretty close to atmospheric pressure, that is 14.7 pounds per square inch, which is the weight of a column of air at sea level on an ideal day.

The purpose of this gauge is to provide you with a relative measure of the performance of your turbocharger. Obviously, the more densified the air entering the combustion chamber of your motor, the more thrust, hence the more power you obtain. At 10,000 feet of altitude (or say 11,018 over the Eisenhower Pass in Colorado) we can only achieve about 10 psia, or 20 in Hg. These mysterious abbreviations are: **psia** = pounds per square inch, absolute, and **in-Hg** = inches of mercury [which is an absolute reading]. One more definition: absolute is a value due to a location such as sea level, or at altitude as opposed to a gauge pressure which might be a reading from an air compressor. Did you understand all that?

So, it is obvious if we only ran our rigs at sea level we would not need a turbocharger and, therefore, no boost gauge.

Basically, this gauge is just something to watch which will give you an indication of your turbocharger's performance. As the turbocharger wears and the bearings get tired, you will probably see a deterioration in the boost pressure. Gauges made for the turbo-charge boost read as both vacuum or pressure gauges. They are calibrated to read from 30 In-Hg (vacuum) to 15 psi (pressure). The port for this gauge would be down stream of the turbocharger and would read in pounds per square inch.

Finally, virtually all vacuum gauges are

mechanical which requires tubing to be connected from the turbocharger to the gauge. This requires careful routing and protection for the tubing. Because of the mechanical nature of this gauge, it is not one frequently seen in conversions.

Pyrometer

The pyrometer, what is it good for, what does it tell you? Many of us install a pyrometer in our instrument cluster because many big rigs have them, but not a lot of us know what its readings indicate. We all know, of course, that the numbers show exhaust gas temperatures, (EGT), but what does that tell us? We'll get into that in a minute.

First, the location of the EGT probe(s) needs to be discussed. These probes, by the way, are nothing more than thermocouples. Most often, an iron-constantan probe is used, which is a combination that generates a micro voltage with temperature changes. This micro voltage is read on a calibrated voltmeter indicating a corresponding temperature. On a naturally aspirated engine, the location of the probe is generally at the first bend in the exhaust manifold, since this will doubtless provide the most sensitive readings. On turbo-charged motors, the probe is customarily located just down stream of the turbo-charger. The reason for this is in the event a probe tip burned loose, or otherwise came loose, it would not plunge into the turbocharger blades, thus rendering the turbocharger a basket case. I have yet to hear of such an event happening, but the logic is sound. In fact, I know of turbocharged engines with the TC probes installed up stream in the elbow positions. However, the downstream position is strongly advised.

Getting back to the meaning of the EGT readings, we know that our fuel contains a specific amount of BTUs, or more simply, heat. Our engines perform most efficiently when we can contain that heat within the combustion chambers. So, the simple answer is to keep our EGT as low as we can, and we will achieve maximum fuel economy. First, understand that the temperature readings we see are generally not absolute, since on a motorhome or a bus conversion, we have to lengthen the leads from our gage to our probe. To minimize voltage drop, we have found that number 12 solid Romax wire serves quite satisfactory, but since we are dealing with microvoltages, we will not read an absolute temperature. This however, is not important, since we are more interested in relative values.

After installing your pyrometer, be sure that you have a clean air filter and fuel filters, so that you can achieve maximum performance. Find a day with little wind, and get up to cruising speed on the flat and level, stabilize, then note your pyrometer reading. This value will be your benchmark for all future conditions. Next, find the toughest grade you can, maintaining the maximum speed you can, and note the reading, This should be your "not-to-exceed" value.

In practice, you will find, that if you are experiencing a head wind, your pyrometer will be elevated. With a tail wind you may even see a value less than your benchmark number. When you are climbing a grade, you will always see an increase in your EGT. Quite often, you can back your foot off the fuel pedal and see a lessening of the EGT, but no drop in RPM. That would be a sure indicator that you were dumping excess fuel out your tailpipe that was of no benefit to your performance. Sometimes, while pulling a grade, it is a real challenge to force your foot to back off the accelerator pedal, but if you can do it and still maintain your engine speed, you are definitely optimizing your fuel economy. See what happens when you go down a grade with your foot off the pedal . . . your pyrometer will be at it's minimum.

If you gradually notice an increased reading while at level cruising, this can be a strong indicator that your air filter is getting dirty and needs changing. An additional indicator that the air filter is dirty, will be black smoke from your exhaust. Keep in mind that black smoke is an indication of unburned fuel, which heats up your exhaust pipes as it leaves the motor.

Getting back to the installation, on a naturally aspirated "V" style engine, it is customary to install two probes at the first elbow in the exhaust manifolds. When this is done, usually a dual pyrometer is installed, and can be used to track the performance of each side of the motor. Each bank should read within about fifty degrees of each other. Under ideal conditions and installation precision, they would read the same on a perfect engine, but there will always be a slight difference. No other wiring except lighting is run to the pyrometer since it is completely actuated by the thermoelectric voltage.

To summarize, the pyrometer is probably your best gage to maintain fuel economy, but you have to read what it's trying to tell you.

Voltmeter

A gauge I consider essential is the voltmeter. These are available in the standard 2 inch diameter size and blend in with the rest of your gauges.

This meter is always connected to your batteries and not only tells you the condition of your starting batteries but will also indicate whether your generator, or alternator are functioning properly.

There are a myriad of ways an electrical system can be installed. At one time, I wired my bus as a 240 VAC system and installed my inverter on one leg which supplied convenience outlets, lamps, microwave oven, and (unfortunately) one roof air conditioning unit. In the heat of traveling through the Las Vegas desert, we turned on our generator to supply AC power to the air conditioners. At that time the generator was installed where its cooling was inadequate and being equipped with murphy gauges (discussed later), it shut itself off. With the generator off, the only AC power came from the inverter and although a 2.5kw inverter would power the air conditioner, it proceeded to suck the batteries dry of power. I discovered this fact from my dash mounted voltmeter as it was reading only about 10 volts DC. The remedy, of course, was to turn off the air conditioner, thus eliminating the demand for AC power. Within in a very few minutes, the alternator brought the batteries up to their normal reading.

Some of you may have retained the original bus generator which is rated at about 280 amps. In my case, I had replaced that huge power stealing generator with a small truck style 105 amp single wire alternator. With the original generator, which on the Eagle is designed to not only power all the lighting throughout the night, but to drive 2-1 horsepower DC motors, it would be a simple task to operate an air conditioner through an inverter.

An average air conditioner has a running power consumption of about 17 amps at 120 volts. This translates to around 180 amps at 12 volt before conversion to AC. Obviously, my simple little 105 ampere alternator would not do the job, thus depleting my batteries.

Incidentally, this gauge is not recommended for your house batteries.

Air Pressure Gauges

Air pressure gauges are essential information on any coach with air brakes. And, I am not aware of many buses without air brakes. In the first place, you must have a minimum of air pressure to unlock your parking brakes. This is so you will have sufficient air pressure to actuate your brakes after you begin to move. Logical?

Most of the air pressure gauges installed in buses are of the dual style. This means they have two connecting fittings and two indicator needles. One needle will point to the bus air pressure stored in the tanks while the other needle will only indicate when the brakes are applied showing the brake application pressure. This figure can be useful when feathering your brakes as you descend a grade.

It used to be common practice, when descending a grade in a big rig without Jake brakes, to hold something like 7 to 10 psi brake pressure in order to maintain control and not over-speed. The more recent accepted technique, however, is to apply sufficient brake pressure to abruptly reduce your speed to a comfortable level and then permit it to build up again. This technique creates a lot of friction and heat on the brakes, but allows a longer cooling time between application. The other technique of holding a constant 7 to 10 psi actually adds a level of heat to the brake drums without a chance to cool and recover.

Obviously, air pressure gauges are mechanical. They are supplied with either metallic tubing such as copper, steel, or aluminum, or DOT nylon plastic tubing. The approved black nylon tubing is quite strong and reliable and easy to install. The same fittings may be used as with metallic tubing with only the addition of an inserted brass sleeve into the end of the plastic tube. As an example, it is possible to replace every air line throughout a coach using the existing fittings by substituting the same size nylon tube with the sleeve inserts. Do not try to use polyethylene tubing in any application, since it does not have the same strength and heat resistance nylon has.

Altimeter

An altimeter is strictly an optional gauge and is mostly just for fun. It really does not tell you anything since regardless of what you do you are going to be only about 5 feet off the ground level while in the driver's seat.

I have an altimeter in my bus only because I'm an old ex-airplane driver and it is comforting to see this particular gauge. In actuality, it's kind of fun to observe your height above sea level. In addition, most altimeters have a built in barometer for adjustment which can provide you with an indication of the type of weather you might expect.

The standard FAA certified altimeter can be pretty expensive plus it will often permit readings exceeding the height of Mount Everest— a little more capacity than needed. I recommend the altimeter built for the new breed of ultra-light aircraft. These altimeters will read up to about 5,500 feet, have a barometric setting capability and only cost about $100. Of course, when traveling over the plains of Utah, exceeding 7,700, feet I have to interpolate.

Several cheaper automotive altimeters are available, but their readings are so course it is hard to determine your elevation within several hundred feet. Even though this could be fatal in an aircraft, it's O.K. in a motor coach, but I still prefer my ultra-light airplane altimeter.

The installation of an altimeter requires absolutely no sender or other hookups. In fact there is not even a light bulb insert point for night illumination. If you are an elevation freak and drive at night, you just may have to install the old fashioned light aircraft red instrument lamp.

Compass

The compass falls into the same category as the altimeter. It's kind of this way. If you are going to stay on the roads (and this is recommended), you are going to be pointing which ever way the roads point. However, I too, have a compass because I like to know which way the road points. In fact, once in Canada, I became suspicious I may be going the wrong direction. My trusty compass alerted me I was heading for the Northwest Territory when all I wanted to do was get to Detroit.

A simple magnetic compass is about all that is really useful. And, they are relatively inexpensive. If you want a flush-dash mounted compass, it can be obtained at almost any airport instrument shop. They are generally mounted in a dampening fluid.

A gyrocompass is not a practical thing in a coach since they tend to progress and must be reset often. This would especially be true as our roads are seldom in a straight line. In addition they require a source of DC power.

A rectangular, dash mounted, electrically powered compass is available for the automotive field. This makes a neat installation and has the advantage of a remote sensor. The biggest problem associated with any compass installation is the influence of magnetic fields near the unit. In addition, since there is so much steel involved in the construction of our rigs, it is difficult to place the compass or the sensor in such a place as to not be affected by the steel. This problem is mitigated in an airplane since much of the structure is aluminum and does not attract the magnetic needle. In all aircraft installations, it is common practice to “swing” the compass. This is a procedure where the airplane is pointed at each of the four compass points and the instrument is adjusted with magnets to maximize the reading accuracy.

This again is an instrument which needs no additional hookups unless you have a remote sensor and it requires a 12VDC source.

An inexpensive compass is available from any automotive supply store and will probably do the job just fine. In this area, there is a broad spectrum of products from which to choose.

Generator Gauges

Instruments for your generator are not, in my humble opinion, really too important. This is especially true if your generator is equipped with low oil pressure and high temperature shut down switches. A typical name for one of these devices is *Alarmastat.* This is nothing more than a temperature sensor with a built-in switch to either open a circuit or close a circuit or both.

If the unit has both, the closing side switch can be connected to a buzzer, or alarm, and the side connected to the opening switch, can connect to the skinner valve or ignition, thus shutting down the motor.

The other type of *Alarmastat* is similar to an oil pressure sender which again, opens a switch, closes a switch or both. It again, is used in the manner described above.

Murphy Gauges

Another useful form of gauge for your generator is known as the Murphy Gauge. This is an instrument which reads like a normal gauge but has a re-settable needle that may be placed at any reading. It is normally set to just above the maximum operating value for the temperature and just below the lowest oil pressure value. If any of the conditions are exceeded, the gauge has a built-in switch that operates in the manner described above in the *Alarmastat* paragraph.

These are useful for machinery which should be monitored occasionally but are not in a convenient location for continuous monitoring. The equipment may be left unattended for long periods of time, fully protected in the event of overheating or loss of oil pressure.

AC Detector

A device known as an AC Detector sounds like a very mysterious piece of equipment. In fact, what I am referring to is really some form of indicator to let you know when you are plugged into shore power. Now, you may rightly ask, "Why do I need to know that? Can't I see the plug as I shove it into the receptacle?" The answer is sure, but have you picked a hot socket? Is the circuit breaker on? Do you want to crawl into your rig and turn on something to test your power? Believe me. This is a very useful device.

It may be as simple as a 120 VAC lamp, or you could actually install a 120 VAC meter near your shore power line to see just how much voltage you are getting.

If you have installed an inverter with a remote control panel mounted at a convenient location inside the coach, it includes a lamp to indicate that AC is detected. Again, however, if you are outside connecting to shore power, it would be convenient to know if you are, in fact, attached to a hot circuit.

This is also useful in case you have kids or dogs playing nearby. These small creatures have an incredible talent for disconnecting RVs from shore power.

The installation is a simple matter of joining a hot lead and a common to your meter or a lamp which can be switched on or off since there is no need to let the lamp burn except when you are monitoring your shore power connection.

Battery Bank Monitor

There are several really neat gadgets which will display the condition of your battery system. Most of these were developed for the yacht and marine industry. One trade name is the *Bank Manager*, whose home location is Seattle, Washington.

Another unit developed specifically for the RV industry is called the *Battery Manager* marketed by RV Power Products (1-800-493-7877). Two options are available. One option is simply a monitor while the other is a battery charger and a remote monitor.

The monitor will display your battery voltage, DC current draw, and, most important, the remaining battery capacity displayed in percentage of a full charge. This allows you to ascertain the general health of your house batteries and 12 volt electrical system. The company claims a plus or minus 5 percent accuracy on battery capacity and one-tenth percent accuracy on the volt meter.

Their battery charger uses a three stage charge process to properly maintain a fully charged battery set without excessive water loss. The bulk charging process applies a 60 amp current at 13.5 volts to quickly bring the batteries up to charge. After this a temperature compensated acceptance voltage is applied. When the current decreases to 1 amp per 100 amp-hours capacity, the system is charged without being overcharged. Finally, a float charge is applied to maintain a fully charged state without excessive water loss and is adjusted continuously, based on battery temperature.

This is one monitor which I consider very useful since it gives you peace of mind as you sit along side that beautiful fishing creek. It will alert you as when you need to crank up your generator, otherwise, you might be running that noisy damned thing unnecessarily. Apologies to generator freaks and those who have a quiet generator installation.

Temperature Gauges

One device I really like, is an ambient temperature gauge. Although often there is little you can do about it, it is comforting to know what the inside and outside temperatures are.

Many times we have been traveling through the Las Vegas desert in the late after noon heading west. While my wife is back in the coach enjoying the cooling air conditioner, I am up in the cockpit sitting in a greenhouse. I will often state with authority the outside temperature is 114° F. and complain the inside temperature where I am sitting is down to 106° F. Although there isn't much I can do about it, short of pointing the coach in the other direction (not an option), I feel properly justified to make these declarations with a degree of martyrdom. Obviously, without a temperature gauge, I would have to suffer in silence; not a happy option.

Perhaps, the simplest and least expense unit, is marketed by Radio Shack. This simple little unit is about 2 inches square and about ¼ inch thick. It uses a watch battery which will last for a couple of years. It has a probe with about ten feet of lead and will read both inside and outside temperature. And, its cost is only about $10 to $15 depending on whether there is a sale.

Although the Radio Shack model is one

product, a variety of this type of gauge are available. Some are designed to flush mount with leads long enough to be placed in strategic locations.

In addition to inside and outside temperature, the refrigerator temperature may also be monitored. You may wonder why this might be important. The RV refrigerator, using the absorption type cooling system, tends to become colder and colder until it becomes a freezer. This makes pouring your milk is little hard (frozen, that is). With a temperature monitor in your refrigerator, the unit can be adjusted periodically.

Besides, when your rig is cool on a hot day, with a thermometer, you just might have bragging rights over your neighbor.

Tank Monitors

Monitors for your fresh water and holding tanks are available in many different forms. Perhaps, the simplest and most reliable is the old fashion fuel gauge using a broken arm float sender with a read out gauge. Then it is a simple matter to have a label engraved and glued over the word fuel. In fact, VDO manufacturers a gauge that just reads *Tank* and another one which is labeled *Water*. These gauges are listed in their marine instruments catalog no. 4452.

This type of tank monitor gauge is unquestionably the most professional installation. Many other tank monitors are also available for the RV industry.

A typical monitor sensor is the type using molded in screw terminals at various levels of the tank. DC current is applied to the bottom terminal and the current is permitted to pass through the liquid level making contact with the top most immersed terminal, lighting a small lamp in the monitor. This is a form of monitor which can be made by almost anyone. It will only work, however, in nonmetallic tanks. such as ones made of polyethylene, polypropolene, fiberglass, or plywood.

Another form of monitor sender which is usable on nonmetallic tanks, uses a metallic film bonded to the outside of the tank. This from of sensor employs the capacitance of the film as sensed through the tank wall. No physical penetration through the tank wall is required.

In metallic tanks, beside using the

typical fuel gauge type of unit, perhaps, the simplest form of gauge is the sight tube. This uses two elbow compression fittings welded to the top and bottom of the tank with a sight glass between. Clear plastic can be just as effective for determining the liquid level and is much safer in a moving vehicle.

With regard to a sight gage, in a semitransparent plastic tank, the liquid level can often be seen by just looking at the tank. If the tank is encased behind a wall, a slot can be made in the wall revealing the liquid level

Propane Gauges

My personal experience with propane gauges has been disappointing. I have used a gauge that is nothing more than a pressure gauge which really does not reveal the amount of gas in the tank. These are after market gauges which may be placed between the tank outlet port, then connected to the supply line.

Another form of gauge is a proper liquid level gauge which must be installed when the tank is manufactured. This is the form I currently have, but even this form of gauge is not very accurate. For this reason, I advocate the use of two tanks with a switchable valve so when one tank is depleted, the reserve tank may take over. Then the primary may be refilled and become the reserve tank. This, of course, assumes you have installed removable tanks.

Backup Monitor

Although a backup monitor and camera is not, strictly speaking, a gauge, it is, nevertheless, a very useful item. And, as such, it should be included in this book.

The term *backup camera* has become commonplace, but a more accurate term might be rear view monitor. It is a quite rare motor-home which has a rear window and since our rear view mirrors are unable to see around corners, this little device solves the problem.

Several very sophisticated units are available. *Intec* was probably one of the first units marketed. This system has a series of dots superimposed over the television screen to indicate distance behind the vehicle. In addition, these dots converge to indicate the clearance on each side of the vehicle. This is quite useful when maneuvering in close quarters. *Sony* markets a competing unit called the Clarion.

Inexpensive systems are also available using small 5" monitors. These are basically designed as security monitors but can be installed in a motorhome. Many of these units have a switchable camera so the image may be reversed and will operate on 12 volts DC. This will then allow you to mount the monitor up by the cockpit and be able to view the rear of the bus as you would through a mirror.

Back in the early days for those coaches with rear windows, a flat plastic screen could be mounted on the rear window which would display a fish-eye type view through your inside rear view mirror.

Safety

Enough can not be said about safety. We should always set aside time to check levels of oil, water and tire pressures to assure that we get to our destination safely. I also consider fire protection to be high on my safety list. I have three ABC dry chemical fire extinguishers in my motorhome (from Costco). One is by the front door, another is in the bedroom (for a good night sleep) and the third is located in an outside storage bay, at the opposite end from the propane tank. I also check that the emergency exit release mechanism works. At least once a year a maintenance check of the entire coach should be performed, from front to back and inside and out. This should also include all hoses, belts and electrical wiring. A little time spent doing these checks will mean many happy miles going down the road.

Lon Cross is a Senior Design Engineer at *The Skunkworks*, birthplace of the famous U2 spy-plane and many other advanced aircraft. Lon's father was an *Oil Man* so they traveled to many exciting places for exploration and production, while residing in a twenty-seven foot trailer.

After a tour of duty in Viet Nam, Lon started his career with Lockheed Aircraft Company. He and his wife Sher bought a used motor coach which had more conveniences than the trailer he grew up in.

Lon served as the President of the largest chapter in FMCA, the California Chapter. In their latest motorhome, he and Sher are still exploring our country,

Appendix

Motor Coach Purchase Check List

Exterior

Siding
Headlights
Marker Lights
Bumpers
Baggage Doors
Windows
Paint
Graphics
Awnings
Hitch
Ladder
Roof Rack
Storage Pad
Back Up Camera
TV Antenna
Satellite Dish

Mechanicals

Engine
Size
Mileage
Cooling System
Transmission
Steering
Wheels
Tires
Brakes
Shocks

Plumbing

Holding Tanks
Dump Valves
Water Pump
Lines
Accumulator
Hose Reel
Water Spray
Filter
Purifier
Fixtures

Electrical

120 V System
12/24 V System
Umbilical
Panel
Monitor

Inverter
Converter
Generator
Batteries
Charging System
Solar Panels

Heating

Forced Air
Catalytic
Ducted
Thermostat
Venting

Air Conditioning

Roof Mounted
Split Airs
Central Air
Bus Air
Dash Air

Ventilation

Roof Vents
Sky Lights
Hatch

Cab

Instruments
Windows
Windshield
Floor
Jake Brake
Power Seat
Cruise Control
Tilt Wheel
AM/FM Cassette
CD Player
CB Radio
Cell Phone
GPS

Living Area

Head liner
Walls
Glass
Chairs
Sofa(s)
Flooring
TV/CD/Stereo
VCR
Lighting
Decking
Dinette
Shades

Light Switches

Galley

Cabinets
Counter Top
Storage
Refrigerator
Range
Ice Maker
Microwave
Sink
Faucet
Pantry
Coffee Maker
Washer/Dryer
Vacuum
Compactor
Floor
Dishwasher
Food Processor

Bathroom

Floor
Head liner
Lighting
Shower/Tub
Jacuzzi
Faucets
Lavatory
Counter Top
Toilet

Closet

Storage
Lighting
Drawers

Bedroom

Floor
Head liner
Lighting
Bed
Bedding
Mattress
TV
Reading Lights

Impressions:

____

____

____

____

____

Bus Conversion Companies

B & B Coachworks
Las Vegas, NV

BCI Coachworks
N.Palm Springs, CA

Beaver
Bend, OR

Country Coach
Junction City, OR

CustomLand Yachts
Windham, ME

Custom Coach
Columbus, OH

Dixieland Conversions
Sevierville, TN

Liberty Coach
Chicago, IL

Lone Wolf Design
Eugene, OR

Marathon
Coburg, OR

Monaco
Coburg, OR

Newell Coach
Miami, OK

Pro Bus
Long Beach, CA

Southwestern Coach
Copeland, KS

Sundance Coach
St. George, UT

Vantare
Sanford, FL

Towing Laws per State						
State	Speed Limit	Length	Width	Height	Max Length	Max Weight
Alabama	55	40'	8'-6"	13'-6"	60'	3,000
Alaska	55	40'	14'	14'	65'	5,000
Arizona	65	40'	8'-6	13'-6"	65'	3,000
Arkansas	65	N/A	8'-6	13'-6"	N/A	3,000
California	55	40'	8'-6	14'	65'	1,500
Colorado	55	57'-4"	8'-6	13'	70'	3,000
Connecticut	55	48'	8'-6	13'-6"	60'	3,000
Delaware	55	40'	8'-6	13'-6"	60'	4,000
Florida	65	N/A	8'-6	13'-6"	60'	3,000
Georgia	65	53'	8'-6	13'-6"	65	2,500
Hawaii	55	40'	9"	14'	60'	3,000
Idaho	65	48"	8'-6	14'	75"	1,500
Illinois	55	42'	8'-6	13'-6"	60'	3,000
Indiana	65	40'	8'-6	13'-6"	60'	3,000
Iowa	65	48'	8'-6	13'-6"	60'	3,000
Kansas	65	N/A	8'-6	14'	65'	N/A
Kentucky	65	N/A	8'-6	13'-6"	55'	N/A
Loiusiana	65	40'	8'-6	13'-6"	N/A	3,000
Maine	65	45'	8'-6	13'-6"	65'	3,000
Mass.	55	40'	8'-6	13'-6"	60'	10,000

Appendix

Towing Laws per State(Continued)						
State	Speed Limit	Length	Width	Height	Max Length	Max Weight
Michigan	65	45'	8'-6"	13'-6"	65'	3,000
Minnesota	65	45'	8'-6"	13'-6"	65'	3,000
Miss.	65	40'	8'-6"	13'-6"	N/A	2,000
Missouri	65	N/A	8'-6"	14'	65'	N/A
Montana	65	45'	8'-6"	14'	75'	3,000
Nebraska	65	40'	8'-6"	14'-6"	65'	3,000
Nevada	65	40'	8'-6"	14'	70'	1,500
N. Hamp.	65	40'	8'-6"	13'-6"	N/A	1,500
N. Jersey	55	35'	8'	13'-6"	50'	3,000
N.Mexico	65	40'	8'-6"	14'	65'	3,000
N. York	55	53'	8'-6"	13'-6"	65'	3,000
N. Carolina	65	40'	8'-6"	13'-6"	60'	1,000
N. Dakota	65	53'	8'-6"	14'	75'	All
Ohio	65	40'	8'-6"	13'-6"	65'	2,000
Oklahoma	65	59.5'	8'-6"	13'-6"	70'	3,000
Oregon	65	35'	8'-6"	14'	50'	3,000
Penn.	55	53'	8'	13'-6"	35'	3,000
R. Island	55	40'	8'-6"	13'-6"	60'	4,000

Towing Laws per State(Continued)						
State	Speed Limit	Length	Width	Height	Max Length	Max Weight
S. Carolina	65	53'	8'-6"	13'-6"	N/A	3,000
S. Dakota	65	53'	8'-6"	14'	70'	3,000
Tenn.	65	50'	8'-6"	13'-6"	65'	3,000
Texas	60	N/A	8'-6"	13'-6"	55'	4,500
Utah	65	45'	8'-6"	13'-6"	65'	2,000
Vermont	65	48'	8'-6"	14'	60'	3,000
Virginia	55	N/A	8'	13'-6"	60'	3,000
Wash.	60	40'	8'-6"	14'	75'	3,000
W. Virginia	65	N/A	8'-6"	13'-6"	55'	3,000
Wisconsin	65	40'	8'-6"	13'-6"	65'	All

See pages 166 and 167 for an explanation of state towing laws.

Index

Symbols

A

B

D

E

F

G

H

R

S

Index

Index

Other Books by Winlock Galey
for the Motor Coaching Gang
by Dave Galey

The Bus Converters's Bible

Classy Cabinets for Converter Coaches

Eagle Planning Sheets

Fascinating Fastener Facts

The Gospel of Gauges

The Joys of Busing

Replacement Electrical Control Panel
Plans & Diagram

Slide out Rooms
Mechanics & Structures

Non Motor Coaching Books

The Grand Assembly
Mary Galey

Shipping Semen for Equine Breeding
Pennie Ahmed

Desert Winds
D. Gordon Johnston

Lethal Mutation
D. Gordon Johnston

Spiritual Truths
Sam Galey

The Grief of Wurzburg
Rose Heide Kolcz